THIS BOOK BELONGS TO:

Name:

Phone:

Email:

IMPORTANT CONTACTS

NAME	JOB	PHONE

IMPORTANT DATES

DATE	NOTES AND REMINDERS

1

PROPERTY INFORMATION

ADDRESS					
BEDROOMS		BATHROOMS		Sq. Ft.	
LOT SIZE		YEAR BUILT		SCHOOL DISTRICT	
ANNUAL TAX		PRICE			

REALTOR INFORMATION

NAME	
AGENCY	
PHONE	
EMAIL	

NOTES AND REMINDERS

INSPECTION CHECKLIST

INTERIOR

FLOORING, WINDOWS & CEILING

FLOOR

☐ Age?

☐ Condition? _____________

WINDOWS

☐ Condition? _____________

CEILING

☐ Condition? _____________

ROOMS

Y N

☐☐ Natural Lighting?

☐☐ Even Floors?

☐☐ Smoke Detectors?

☐☐ Carbon Monoxide Detector?

WALLS

Y N

☐☐ Stains?

☐☐ Need Re-painting?

☐☐ Soundproof?

STAIRS

Y N

☐☐ Creaky?

☐☐ Signs of Damage?

DOORS

Y N

☐☐ Open & Close Property

☐☐ Weather Proofed

☐☐ Working Doorbell

BATHROOM

Y N

☐☐ Stain-free?

☐☐ Mildew/Mold-free?

☐☐ Leak-free?

☐☐ Cabinet & Storage Space?

☐☐ Working Fans?

☐☐ Functioning Toilet?

KITCHEN

Y N

☐☐ Stain-free?

☐☐ Mildew/Mold-free?

☐☐ Leak-free?

☐☐ Cabinet & Storage Space?

☐☐ Working Fans?

☐☐ Working Garbage Disposal?

EXTERIOR

UP-TO-DATE SYSTEMS

☐ Hire Home Inspector [*before purchase*]

☐ Electrical

☐ A/C

☐ Heating

☐ Security

☐ Plumbing

☐ Water

☐ Sewer Insulation

ROOF

Y N

☐☐ Sagging Roof Line?

☐☐ Discoloration?

☐☐ Holes?

FOUNDATION, DRIVEWAY, & POOL

FOUNDATION

☐ Visible Cracks? _____________

DRIVEWAY

☐ Visible Cracks? _____________

POOL

☐ Visible Cracks? _____________

☐ Above Ground? _____________

GARAGE

Y N

☐☐ Functional - Manual?

☐☐ Functional - Remote?

☐ N/A

SIDING

Y N

☐☐ Paint Peeling?

☐☐ Cracks/Splits?

LANDSCAPING & CURB APPEAL

☐ Trees - Condition?

____

☐ Lawn [*front*] - Condition?

____

☐ Lawn [*back*] - Condition?

____

☐ Fences - Condition?

____

☐ Landscaping - Condition?

____

2

PROPERTY INFORMATION

ADDRESS	
BEDROOMS		BATHROOMS		Sq. Ft.	
LOT SIZE		YEAR BUILT		SCHOOL DISTRICT	
ANNUAL TAX		PRICE	

REALTOR INFORMATION

NAME	
AGENCY	
PHONE	
EMAIL	

NOTES AND REMINDERS

INSPECTION CHECKLIST

INTERIOR

FLOORING, WINDOWS & CEILING

FLOOR

☐ Age?

☐ Condition? _____________

WINDOWS

☐ Condition? _____________

CEILING

☐ Condition? _____________

ROOMS

Y N

☐☐ Natural Lighting?

☐☐ Even Floors?

☐☐ Smoke Detectors?

☐☐ Carbon Monoxide Detector?

WALLS

Y N

☐☐ Stains?

☐☐ Need Re-painting?

☐☐ Soundproof?

STAIRS

Y N

☐☐ Creaky?

☐☐ Signs of Damage?

DOORS

Y N

☐☐ Open & Close Property

☐☐ Weather Proofed

☐☐ Working Doorbell

BATHROOM

Y N

☐☐ Stain-free?

☐☐ Mildew/Mold-free?

☐☐ Leak-free?

☐☐ Cabinet & Storage Space?

☐☐ Working Fans?

☐☐ Functioning Toilet?

KITCHEN

Y N

☐☐ Stain-free?

☐☐ Mildew/Mold-free?

☐☐ Leak-free?

☐☐ Cabinet & Storage Space?

☐☐ Working Fans?

☐☐ Working Garbage Disposal?

EXTERIOR

UP-TO-DATE SYSTEMS

☐ Hire Home Inspector [*before purchase*]

☐ Electrical

☐ A/C

☐ Heating

☐ Security

☐ Plumbing

☐ Water

☐ Sewer Insulation

ROOF

Y N

☐☐ Sagging Roof Line?

☐☐ Discoloration?

☐☐ Holes?

FOUNDATION, DRIVEWAY, & POOL

FOUNDATION

☐ Visible Cracks? _____________

DRIVEWAY

☐ Visible Cracks? _____________

POOL

☐ Visible Cracks? _____________

☐ Above Ground? _____________

GARAGE

Y N

☐☐ Functional - Manual?

☐☐ Functional - Remote?

☐ N/A

SIDING

Y N

☐☐ Paint Peeling?

☐☐ Cracks/Splits?

LANDSCAPING & CURB APPEAL

☐ Trees - Condition?

____

☐ Lawn [*front*] - Condition?

____

☐ Lawn [*back*] - Condition?

____

☐ Fences - Condition?

____

☐ Landscaping - Condition?

____

3

PROPERTY INFORMATION

ADDRESS					
BEDROOMS		BATHROOMS		Sq. Ft.	
LOT SIZE		YEAR BUILT		SCHOOL DISTRICT	
ANNUAL TAX		PRICE			

REALTOR INFORMATION

NAME	
AGENCY	
PHONE	
EMAIL	

NOTES AND REMINDERS

INSPECTION CHECKLIST

INTERIOR

FLOORING, WINDOWS & CEILING

FLOOR

☐ Age?

☐ Condition? ___________

WINDOWS

☐ Condition? ___________

CEILING

☐ Condition? ___________

ROOMS

Y N

☐☐ Natural Lighting?

☐☐ Even Floors?

☐☐ Smoke Detectors?

☐☐ Carbon Monoxide Detector?

WALLS

Y N

☐☐ Stains?

☐☐ Need Re-painting?

☐☐ Soundproof?

STAIRS

Y N

☐☐ Creaky?

☐☐ Signs of Damage?

DOORS

Y N

☐☐ Open & Close Property

☐☐ Weather Proofed

☐☐ Working Doorbell

BATHROOM

Y N

☐☐ Stain-free?

☐☐ Mildew/Mold-free?

☐☐ Leak-free?

☐☐ Cabinet & Storage Space?

☐☐ Working Fans?

☐☐ Functioning Toilet?

KITCHEN

Y N

☐☐ Stain-free?

☐☐ Mildew/Mold-free?

☐☐ Leak-free?

☐☐ Cabinet & Storage Space?

☐☐ Working Fans?

☐☐ Working Garbage Disposal?

EXTERIOR

UP-TO-DATE SYSTEMS

☐ Hire Home Inspector [*before purchase*]

☐ Electrical

☐ A/C

☐ Heating

☐ Security

☐ Plumbing

☐ Water

☐ Sewer Insulation

ROOF

Y N

☐☐ Sagging Roof Line?

☐☐ Discoloration?

☐☐ Holes?

FOUNDATION, DRIVEWAY, & POOL

FOUNDATION

☐ Visible Cracks? ___________

DRIVEWAY

☐ Visible Cracks? ___________

POOL

☐ Visible Cracks? ___________

☐ Above Ground? ___________

GARAGE

Y N

☐☐ Functional - Manual?

☐☐ Functional - Remote?

☐ N/A

SIDING

Y N

☐☐ Paint Peeling?

☐☐ Cracks/Splits?

LANDSCAPING & CURB APPEAL

☐ Trees - Condition?

____

☐ Lawn [*front*] - Condition?

____

☐ Lawn [*back*] - Condition?

____

☐ Fences - Condition?

____

☐ Landscaping - Condition?

____

4

PROPERTY INFORMATION

ADDRESS	

BEDROOMS		BATHROOMS		Sq. Ft.	
LOT SIZE		YEAR BUILT		SCHOOL DISTRICT	
ANNUAL TAX		PRICE			

REALTOR INFORMATION

NAME	
AGENCY	
PHONE	
EMAIL	

NOTES AND REMINDERS

INSPECTION CHECKLIST

INTERIOR

FLOORING, WINDOWS & CEILING

FLOOR
- ☐ Age?
- ☐ Condition? ______________

WINDOWS
- ☐ Condition? ______________

CEILING
- ☐ Condition? ______________

ROOMS

Y N
- ☐☐ Natural Lighting?
- ☐☐ Even Floors?
- ☐☐ Smoke Detectors?
- ☐☐ Carbon Monoxide Detector?

WALLS

Y N
- ☐☐ Stains?
- ☐☐ Need Re-painting?
- ☐☐ Soundproof?

STAIRS

Y N
- ☐☐ Creaky?
- ☐☐ Signs of Damage?

DOORS

Y N
- ☐☐ Open & Close Property
- ☐☐ Weather Proofed
- ☐☐ Working Doorbell

BATHROOM

Y N
- ☐☐ Stain-free?
- ☐☐ Mildew/Mold-free?
- ☐☐ Leak-free?
- ☐☐ Cabinet & Storage Space?
- ☐☐ Working Fans?
- ☐☐ Functioning Toilet?

KITCHEN

Y N
- ☐☐ Stain-free?
- ☐☐ Mildew/Mold-free?
- ☐☐ Leak-free?
- ☐☐ Cabinet & Storage Space?
- ☐☐ Working Fans?
- ☐☐ Working Garbage Disposal?

EXTERIOR

UP-TO-DATE SYSTEMS

- ☐ Hire Home Inspector [*before purchase*]
- ☐ Electrical
- ☐ A/C
- ☐ Heating
- ☐ Security
- ☐ Plumbing
- ☐ Water
- ☐ Sewer Insulation

ROOF

Y N
- ☐☐ Sagging Roof Line?
- ☐☐ Discoloration?
- ☐☐ Holes?

FOUNDATION, DRIVEWAY, & POOL

FOUNDATION
- ☐ Visible Cracks? ______________

DRIVEWAY
- ☐ Visible Cracks? ______________

POOL
- ☐ Visible Cracks? ______________
- ☐ Above Ground? ______________

GARAGE

Y N
- ☐☐ Functional - Manual?
- ☐☐ Functional - Remote?
- ☐ N/A

SIDING

Y N
- ☐☐ Paint Peeling?
- ☐☐ Cracks/Splits?

LANDSCAPING & CURB APPEAL

- ☐ Trees - Condition?
  ____

- ☐ Lawn [*front*] - Condition?
  ____

- ☐ Lawn [*back*] - Condition?
  ____

- ☐ Fences - Condition?
  ____

- ☐ Landscaping - Condition?
  ____

5

PROPERTY INFORMATION

ADDRESS	

BEDROOMS		BATHROOMS		Sq. Ft.	
LOT SIZE		YEAR BUILT		SCHOOL DISTRICT	
ANNUAL TAX		PRICE			

REALTOR INFORMATION

NAME	
AGENCY	
PHONE	
EMAIL	

NOTES AND REMINDERS

INSPECTION CHECKLIST

INTERIOR

FLOORING, WINDOWS & CEILING

FLOOR
- [ ] Age?
- [ ] Condition? ______________

WINDOWS
- [ ] Condition? ______________

CEILING
- [ ] Condition? ______________

ROOMS

Y N
- [ ] [ ] Natural Lighting?
- [ ] [ ] Even Floors?
- [ ] [ ] Smoke Detectors?
- [ ] [ ] Carbon Monoxide Detector?

WALLS

Y N
- [ ] [ ] Stains?
- [ ] [ ] Need Re-painting?
- [ ] [ ] Soundproof?

STAIRS

Y N
- [ ] [ ] Creaky?
- [ ] [ ] Signs of Damage?

DOORS

Y N
- [ ] [ ] Open & Close Property
- [ ] [ ] Weather Proofed
- [ ] [ ] Working Doorbell

BATHROOM

Y N
- [ ] [ ] Stain-free?
- [ ] [ ] Mildew/Mold-free?
- [ ] [ ] Leak-free?
- [ ] [ ] Cabinet & Storage Space?
- [ ] [ ] Working Fans?
- [ ] [ ] Functioning Toilet?

KITCHEN

Y N
- [ ] [ ] Stain-free?
- [ ] [ ] Mildew/Mold-free?
- [ ] [ ] Leak-free?
- [ ] [ ] Cabinet & Storage Space?
- [ ] [ ] Working Fans?
- [ ] [ ] Working Garbage Disposal?

EXTERIOR

UP-TO-DATE SYSTEMS

- [ ] Hire Home Inspector [*before purchase*]
- [ ] Electrical
- [ ] A/C
- [ ] Heating
- [ ] Security
- [ ] Plumbing
- [ ] Water
- [ ] Sewer Insulation

ROOF

Y N
- [ ] [ ] Sagging Roof Line?
- [ ] [ ] Discoloration?
- [ ] [ ] Holes?

FOUNDATION, DRIVEWAY, & POOL

FOUNDATION
- [ ] Visible Cracks? ___________

DRIVEWAY
- [ ] Visible Cracks? ___________

POOL
- [ ] Visible Cracks? ___________
- [ ] Above Ground? ___________

GARAGE

Y N
- [ ] [ ] Functional - Manual?
- [ ] [ ] Functional - Remote?
- [ ] N/A

SIDING

Y N
- [ ] [ ] Paint Peeling?
- [ ] [ ] Cracks/Splits?

LANDSCAPING & CURB APPEAL

- [ ] Trees - Condition?

____

- [ ] Lawn [*front*] - Condition?

____

- [ ] Lawn [*back*] - Condition?

____

- [ ] Fences - Condition?

____

- [ ] Landscaping - Condition?

____

6

PROPERTY INFORMATION

ADDRESS	

BEDROOMS		**BATHROOMS**		**Sq. Ft.**	
LOT SIZE		**YEAR BUILT**		**SCHOOL DISTRICT**	
ANNUAL TAX		**PRICE**			

REALTOR INFORMATION

NAME	
AGENCY	
PHONE	
EMAIL	

NOTES AND REMINDERS

INSPECTION CHECKLIST

INTERIOR

FLOORING, WINDOWS & CEILING

FLOOR

☐ Age?

☐ Condition? ___________

WINDOWS

☐ Condition? ___________

CEILING

☐ Condition? ___________

ROOMS

Y N

☐☐ Natural Lighting?

☐☐ Even Floors?

☐☐ Smoke Detectors?

☐☐ Carbon Monoxide Detector?

WALLS

Y N

☐☐ Stains?

☐☐ Need Re-painting?

☐☐ Soundproof?

STAIRS

Y N

☐☐ Creaky?

☐☐ Signs of Damage?

DOORS

Y N

☐☐ Open & Close Property

☐☐ Weather Proofed

☐☐ Working Doorbell

BATHROOM

Y N

☐☐ Stain-free?

☐☐ Mildew/Mold-free?

☐☐ Leak-free?

☐☐ Cabinet & Storage Space?

☐☐ Working Fans?

☐☐ Functioning Toilet?

KITCHEN

Y N

☐☐ Stain-free?

☐☐ Mildew/Mold-free?

☐☐ Leak-free?

☐☐ Cabinet & Storage Space?

☐☐ Working Fans?

☐☐ Working Garbage Disposal?

EXTERIOR

UP-TO-DATE SYSTEMS

☐ Hire Home Inspector [*before purchase*]

☐ Electrical

☐ A/C

☐ Heating

☐ Security

☐ Plumbing

☐ Water

☐ Sewer Insulation

ROOF

Y N

☐☐ Sagging Roof Line?

☐☐ Discoloration?

☐☐ Holes?

FOUNDATION, DRIVEWAY, & POOL

FOUNDATION

☐ Visible Cracks? __________

DRIVEWAY

☐ Visible Cracks? __________

POOL

☐ Visible Cracks? __________

☐ Above Ground? __________

GARAGE

Y N

☐☐ Functional - Manual?

☐☐ Functional - Remote?

☐ N/A

SIDING

Y N

☐☐ Paint Peeling?

☐☐ Cracks/Splits?

LANDSCAPING & CURB APPEAL

☐ Trees - Condition?

____

☐ Lawn [*front*] - Condition?

____

☐ Lawn [*back*] - Condition?

____

☐ Fences - Condition?

____

☐ Landscaping - Condition?

____

7

PROPERTY INFORMATION

ADDRESS				
BEDROOMS		BATHROOMS		Sq. Ft.
LOT SIZE		YEAR BUILT		SCHOOL DISTRICT
ANNUAL TAX		PRICE		

REALTOR INFORMATION

NAME	
AGENCY	
PHONE	
EMAIL	

NOTES AND REMINDERS

INSPECTION CHECKLIST

INTERIOR

FLOORING, WINDOWS & CEILING

FLOOR
- ☐ Age?
- ☐ Condition? ___________

WINDOWS
- ☐ Condition? ___________

CEILING
- ☐ Condition? ___________

ROOMS

Y N
- ☐☐ Natural Lighting?
- ☐☐ Even Floors?
- ☐☐ Smoke Detectors?
- ☐☐ Carbon Monoxide Detector?

WALLS

Y N
- ☐☐ Stains?
- ☐☐ Need Re-painting?
- ☐☐ Soundproof?

STAIRS

Y N
- ☐☐ Creaky?
- ☐☐ Signs of Damage?

DOORS

Y N
- ☐☐ Open & Close Property
- ☐☐ Weather Proofed
- ☐☐ Working Doorbell

BATHROOM

Y N
- ☐☐ Stain-free?
- ☐☐ Mildew/Mold-free?
- ☐☐ Leak-free?
- ☐☐ Cabinet & Storage Space?
- ☐☐ Working Fans?
- ☐☐ Functioning Toilet?

KITCHEN

Y N
- ☐☐ Stain-free?
- ☐☐ Mildew/Mold-free?
- ☐☐ Leak-free?
- ☐☐ Cabinet & Storage Space?
- ☐☐ Working Fans?
- ☐☐ Working Garbage Disposal?

EXTERIOR

UP-TO-DATE SYSTEMS

- ☐ Hire Home Inspector [*before purchase*]
- ☐ Electrical
- ☐ A/C
- ☐ Heating
- ☐ Security
- ☐ Plumbing
- ☐ Water
- ☐ Sewer Insulation

ROOF

Y N
- ☐☐ Sagging Roof Line?
- ☐☐ Discoloration?
- ☐☐ Holes?

FOUNDATION, DRIVEWAY, & POOL

FOUNDATION
- ☐ Visible Cracks? ___________

DRIVEWAY
- ☐ Visible Cracks? ___________

POOL
- ☐ Visible Cracks? ___________
- ☐ Above Ground? ___________

GARAGE

Y N
- ☐☐ Functional - Manual?
- ☐☐ Functional - Remote?
- ☐ N/A

SIDING

Y N
- ☐☐ Paint Peeling?
- ☐☐ Cracks/Splits?

LANDSCAPING & CURB APPEAL

- ☐ Trees - Condition?

____

- ☐ Lawn [*front*] - Condition?

____

- ☐ Lawn [*back*] - Condition?

____

- ☐ Fences - Condition?

____

- ☐ Landscaping - Condition?

____

8

PROPERTY INFORMATION

ADDRESS					
BEDROOMS		BATHROOMS		Sq. Ft.	
LOT SIZE		YEAR BUILT		SCHOOL DISTRICT	
ANNUAL TAX		PRICE			

REALTOR INFORMATION

NAME	
AGENCY	
PHONE	
EMAIL	

NOTES AND REMINDERS

INSPECTION CHECKLIST

INTERIOR

FLOORING, WINDOWS & CEILING

FLOOR
- ☐ Age?
- ☐ Condition? _____________

WINDOWS
- ☐ Condition? _____________

CEILING
- ☐ Condition? _____________

ROOMS

Y N
- ☐☐ Natural Lighting?
- ☐☐ Even Floors?
- ☐☐ Smoke Detectors?
- ☐☐ Carbon Monoxide Detector?

WALLS

Y N
- ☐☐ Stains?
- ☐☐ Need Re-painting?
- ☐☐ Soundproof?

STAIRS

Y N
- ☐☐ Creaky?
- ☐☐ Signs of Damage?

DOORS

Y N
- ☐☐ Open & Close Property
- ☐☐ Weather Proofed
- ☐☐ Working Doorbell

BATHROOM

Y N
- ☐☐ Stain-free?
- ☐☐ Mildew/Mold-free?
- ☐☐ Leak-free?
- ☐☐ Cabinet & Storage Space?
- ☐☐ Working Fans?
- ☐☐ Functioning Toilet?

KITCHEN

Y N
- ☐☐ Stain-free?
- ☐☐ Mildew/Mold-free?
- ☐☐ Leak-free?
- ☐☐ Cabinet & Storage Space?
- ☐☐ Working Fans?
- ☐☐ Working Garbage Disposal?

EXTERIOR

UP-TO-DATE SYSTEMS

- ☐ Hire Home Inspector [*before purchase*]
- ☐ Electrical
- ☐ A/C
- ☐ Heating
- ☐ Security
- ☐ Plumbing
- ☐ Water
- ☐ Sewer Insulation

ROOF

Y N
- ☐☐ Sagging Roof Line?
- ☐☐ Discoloration?
- ☐☐ Holes?

FOUNDATION, DRIVEWAY, & POOL

FOUNDATION
- ☐ Visible Cracks? _____________

DRIVEWAY
- ☐ Visible Cracks? _____________

POOL
- ☐ Visible Cracks? _____________
- ☐ Above Ground? _____________

GARAGE

Y N
- ☐☐ Functional - Manual?
- ☐☐ Functional - Remote?
- ☐ N/A

SIDING

Y N
- ☐☐ Paint Peeling?
- ☐☐ Cracks/Splits?

LANDSCAPING & CURB APPEAL

- ☐ Trees - Condition?

____

- ☐ Lawn [*front*] - Condition?

____

- ☐ Lawn [*back*] - Condition?

____

- ☐ Fences - Condition?

____

- ☐ Landscaping - Condition?

____

9

PROPERTY INFORMATION

ADDRESS	
BEDROOMS		BATHROOMS		Sq. Ft.	
LOT SIZE		YEAR BUILT		SCHOOL DISTRICT	
ANNUAL TAX		PRICE	

REALTOR INFORMATION

NAME	
AGENCY	
PHONE	
EMAIL	

NOTES AND REMINDERS

INSPECTION CHECKLIST

INTERIOR

FLOORING, WINDOWS & CEILING

FLOOR

☐ Age?

☐ Condition? _____________

WINDOWS

☐ Condition? _____________

CEILING

☐ Condition? _____________

ROOMS

Y N

☐☐ Natural Lighting?

☐☐ Even Floors?

☐☐ Smoke Detectors?

☐☐ Carbon Monoxide Detector?

WALLS

Y N

☐☐ Stains?

☐☐ Need Re-painting?

☐☐ Soundproof?

STAIRS

Y N

☐☐ Creaky?

☐☐ Signs of Damage?

DOORS

Y N

☐☐ Open & Close Property

☐☐ Weather Proofed

☐☐ Working Doorbell

BATHROOM

Y N

☐☐ Stain-free?

☐☐ Mildew/Mold-free?

☐☐ Leak-free?

☐☐ Cabinet & Storage Space?

☐☐ Working Fans?

☐☐ Functioning Toilet?

KITCHEN

Y N

☐☐ Stain-free?

☐☐ Mildew/Mold-free?

☐☐ Leak-free?

☐☐ Cabinet & Storage Space?

☐☐ Working Fans?

☐☐ Working Garbage Disposal?

EXTERIOR

UP-TO-DATE SYSTEMS

☐ Hire Home Inspector [*before purchase*]

☐ Electrical

☐ A/C

☐ Heating

☐ Security

☐ Plumbing

☐ Water

☐ Sewer Insulation

ROOF

Y N

☐☐ Sagging Roof Line?

☐☐ Discoloration?

☐☐ Holes?

FOUNDATION, DRIVEWAY, & POOL

FOUNDATION

☐ Visible Cracks? _____________

DRIVEWAY

☐ Visible Cracks? _____________

POOL

☐ Visible Cracks? _____________

☐ Above Ground? _____________

GARAGE

Y N

☐☐ Functional - Manual?

☐☐ Functional - Remote?

☐ N/A

SIDING

Y N

☐☐ Paint Peeling?

☐☐ Cracks/Splits?

LANDSCAPING & CURB APPEAL

☐ Trees - Condition?

____

☐ Lawn [*front*] - Condition?

____

☐ Lawn [*back*] - Condition?

____

☐ Fences - Condition?

____

☐ Landscaping - Condition?

____

10

PROPERTY INFORMATION

ADDRESS	
BEDROOMS		BATHROOMS		Sq. Ft.	
LOT SIZE		YEAR BUILT		SCHOOL DISTRICT	
ANNUAL TAX		PRICE	

REALTOR INFORMATION

NAME	
AGENCY	
PHONE	
EMAIL	

NOTES AND REMINDERS

INSPECTION CHECKLIST

INTERIOR

FLOORING, WINDOWS & CEILING

FLOOR
- ☐ Age?
- ☐ Condition? ____________

WINDOWS
- ☐ Condition? ____________

CEILING
- ☐ Condition? ____________

ROOMS

Y N
- ☐☐ Natural Lighting?
- ☐☐ Even Floors?
- ☐☐ Smoke Detectors?
- ☐☐ Carbon Monoxide Detector?

WALLS

Y N
- ☐☐ Stains?
- ☐☐ Need Re-painting?
- ☐☐ Soundproof?

STAIRS

Y N
- ☐☐ Creaky?
- ☐☐ Signs of Damage?

DOORS

Y N
- ☐☐ Open & Close Property
- ☐☐ Weather Proofed
- ☐☐ Working Doorbell

BATHROOM

Y N
- ☐☐ Stain-free?
- ☐☐ Mildew/Mold-free?
- ☐☐ Leak-free?
- ☐☐ Cabinet & Storage Space?
- ☐☐ Working Fans?
- ☐☐ Functioning Toilet?

KITCHEN

Y N
- ☐☐ Stain-free?
- ☐☐ Mildew/Mold-free?
- ☐☐ Leak-free?
- ☐☐ Cabinet & Storage Space?
- ☐☐ Working Fans?
- ☐☐ Working Garbage Disposal?

EXTERIOR

UP-TO-DATE SYSTEMS

- ☐ Hire Home Inspector [*before purchase*]
- ☐ Electrical
- ☐ A/C
- ☐ Heating
- ☐ Security
- ☐ Plumbing
- ☐ Water
- ☐ Sewer Insulation

ROOF

Y N
- ☐☐ Sagging Roof Line?
- ☐☐ Discoloration?
- ☐☐ Holes?

FOUNDATION, DRIVEWAY, & POOL

FOUNDATION
- ☐ Visible Cracks? ____________

DRIVEWAY
- ☐ Visible Cracks? ____________

POOL
- ☐ Visible Cracks? ____________
- ☐ Above Ground? ____________

GARAGE

Y N
- ☐☐ Functional - Manual?
- ☐☐ Functional - Remote?
- ☐ N/A

SIDING

Y N
- ☐☐ Paint Peeling?
- ☐☐ Cracks/Splits?

LANDSCAPING & CURB APPEAL

- ☐ Trees - Condition?
____

- ☐ Lawn [*front*] - Condition?
____

- ☐ Lawn [*back*] - Condition?
____

- ☐ Fences - Condition?
____

- ☐ Landscaping - Condition?
____

11

PROPERTY INFORMATION

ADDRESS	
BEDROOMS		BATHROOMS		Sq. Ft.	
LOT SIZE		YEAR BUILT		SCHOOL DISTRICT	
ANNUAL TAX		PRICE	

REALTOR INFORMATION

NAME	
AGENCY	
PHONE	
EMAIL	

NOTES AND REMINDERS

INSPECTION CHECKLIST

INTERIOR

FLOORING, WINDOWS & CEILING

FLOOR

☐ Age?

☐ Condition? ________________

WINDOWS

☐ Condition? ________________

CEILING

☐ Condition? ________________

ROOMS

Y N

☐☐ Natural Lighting?

☐☐ Even Floors?

☐☐ Smoke Detectors?

☐☐ Carbon Monoxide Detector?

WALLS

Y N

☐☐ Stains?

☐☐ Need Re-painting?

☐☐ Soundproof?

STAIRS

Y N

☐☐ Creaky?

☐☐ Signs of Damage?

DOORS

Y N

☐☐ Open & Close Property

☐☐ Weather Proofed

☐☐ Working Doorbell

BATHROOM

Y N

☐☐ Stain-free?

☐☐ Mildew/Mold-free?

☐☐ Leak-free?

☐☐ Cabinet & Storage Space?

☐☐ Working Fans?

☐☐ Functioning Toilet?

KITCHEN

Y N

☐☐ Stain-free?

☐☐ Mildew/Mold-free?

☐☐ Leak-free?

☐☐ Cabinet & Storage Space?

☐☐ Working Fans?

☐☐ Working Garbage Disposal?

EXTERIOR

UP-TO-DATE SYSTEMS

☐ Hire Home Inspector [*before purchase*]

☐ Electrical

☐ A/C

☐ Heating

☐ Security

☐ Plumbing

☐ Water

☐ Sewer Insulation

ROOF

Y N

☐☐ Sagging Roof Line?

☐☐ Discoloration?

☐☐ Holes?

FOUNDATION, DRIVEWAY, & POOL

FOUNDATION

☐ Visible Cracks? ____________

DRIVEWAY

☐ Visible Cracks? ____________

POOL

☐ Visible Cracks? ____________

☐ Above Ground? ____________

GARAGE

Y N

☐☐ Functional - Manual?

☐☐ Functional - Remote?

☐ N/A

SIDING

Y N

☐☐ Paint Peeling?

☐☐ Cracks/Splits?

LANDSCAPING & CURB APPEAL

☐ Trees - Condition?

____

☐ Lawn [*front*] - Condition?

____

☐ Lawn [*back*] - Condition?

____

☐ Fences - Condition?

____

☐ Landscaping - Condition?

____

12

PROPERTY INFORMATION

ADDRESS					
BEDROOMS		**BATHROOMS**		**Sq. Ft.**	
LOT SIZE		**YEAR BUILT**		**SCHOOL DISTRICT**	
ANNUAL TAX		**PRICE**			

REALTOR INFORMATION

NAME	
AGENCY	
PHONE	
EMAIL	

NOTES AND REMINDERS

INSPECTION CHECKLIST

INTERIOR

FLOORING, WINDOWS & CEILING

FLOOR

☐ Age?

☐ Condition? ______________

WINDOWS

☐ Condition? ______________

CEILING

☐ Condition? ______________

ROOMS

Y N

☐☐ Natural Lighting?

☐☐ Even Floors?

☐☐ Smoke Detectors?

☐☐ Carbon Monoxide Detector?

WALLS

Y N

☐☐ Stains?

☐☐ Need Re-painting?

☐☐ Soundproof?

STAIRS

Y N

☐☐ Creaky?

☐☐ Signs of Damage?

DOORS

Y N

☐☐ Open & Close Property

☐☐ Weather Proofed

☐☐ Working Doorbell

BATHROOM

Y N

☐☐ Stain-free?

☐☐ Mildew/Mold-free?

☐☐ Leak-free?

☐☐ Cabinet & Storage Space?

☐☐ Working Fans?

☐☐ Functioning Toilet?

KITCHEN

Y N

☐☐ Stain-free?

☐☐ Mildew/Mold-free?

☐☐ Leak-free?

☐☐ Cabinet & Storage Space?

☐☐ Working Fans?

☐☐ Working Garbage Disposal?

EXTERIOR

UP-TO-DATE SYSTEMS

☐ Hire Home Inspector [*before purchase*]

☐ Electrical

☐ A/C

☐ Heating

☐ Security

☐ Plumbing

☐ Water

☐ Sewer Insulation

ROOF

Y N

☐☐ Sagging Roof Line?

☐☐ Discoloration?

☐☐ Holes?

FOUNDATION, DRIVEWAY, & POOL

FOUNDATION

☐ Visible Cracks? ______________

DRIVEWAY

☐ Visible Cracks? ______________

POOL

☐ Visible Cracks? ______________

☐ Above Ground? ______________

GARAGE

Y N

☐☐ Functional - Manual?

☐☐ Functional - Remote?

☐ N/A

SIDING

Y N

☐☐ Paint Peeling?

☐☐ Cracks/Splits?

LANDSCAPING & CURB APPEAL

☐ Trees - Condition?

____

☐ Lawn [*front*] - Condition?

____

☐ Lawn [*back*] - Condition?

____

☐ Fences - Condition?

____

☐ Landscaping - Condition?

____

13

PROPERTY INFORMATION

ADDRESS	

BEDROOMS		**BATHROOMS**		**Sq. Ft.**	
LOT SIZE		**YEAR BUILT**		**SCHOOL DISTRICT**	
ANNUAL TAX		**PRICE**			

REALTOR INFORMATION

NAME	
AGENCY	
PHONE	
EMAIL	

NOTES AND REMINDERS

INSPECTION CHECKLIST

INTERIOR

FLOORING, WINDOWS & CEILING

FLOOR

☐ Age?

☐ Condition? _____________

WINDOWS

☐ Condition? _____________

CEILING

☐ Condition? _____________

ROOMS

Y N

☐☐ Natural Lighting?

☐☐ Even Floors?

☐☐ Smoke Detectors?

☐☐ Carbon Monoxide Detector?

WALLS

Y N

☐☐ Stains?

☐☐ Need Re-painting?

☐☐ Soundproof?

STAIRS

Y N

☐☐ Creaky?

☐☐ Signs of Damage?

DOORS

Y N

☐☐ Open & Close Property

☐☐ Weather Proofed

☐☐ Working Doorbell

BATHROOM

Y N

☐☐ Stain-free?

☐☐ Mildew/Mold-free?

☐☐ Leak-free?

☐☐ Cabinet & Storage Space?

☐☐ Working Fans?

☐☐ Functioning Toilet?

KITCHEN

Y N

☐☐ Stain-free?

☐☐ Mildew/Mold-free?

☐☐ Leak-free?

☐☐ Cabinet & Storage Space?

☐☐ Working Fans?

☐☐ Working Garbage Disposal?

EXTERIOR

UP-TO-DATE SYSTEMS

☐ Hire Home Inspector [*before purchase*]

☐ Electrical

☐ A/C

☐ Heating

☐ Security

☐ Plumbing

☐ Water

☐ Sewer Insulation

ROOF

Y N

☐☐ Sagging Roof Line?

☐☐ Discoloration?

☐☐ Holes?

FOUNDATION, DRIVEWAY, & POOL

FOUNDATION

☐ Visible Cracks? _____________

DRIVEWAY

☐ Visible Cracks? _____________

POOL

☐ Visible Cracks? _____________

☐ Above Ground? _____________

GARAGE

Y N

☐☐ Functional - Manual?

☐☐ Functional - Remote?

☐ N/A

SIDING

Y N

☐☐ Paint Peeling?

☐☐ Cracks/Splits?

LANDSCAPING & CURB APPEAL

☐ Trees - Condition?

____

☐ Lawn [*front*] - Condition?

____

☐ Lawn [*back*] - Condition?

____

☐ Fences - Condition?

____

☐ Landscaping - Condition?

____

14

PROPERTY INFORMATION

ADDRESS	
BEDROOMS		BATHROOMS		Sq. Ft.	
LOT SIZE		YEAR BUILT		SCHOOL DISTRICT	
ANNUAL TAX		PRICE	

REALTOR INFORMATION

NAME	
AGENCY	
PHONE	
EMAIL	

NOTES AND REMINDERS

INSPECTION CHECKLIST

INTERIOR

FLOORING, WINDOWS & CEILING

FLOOR

☐ Age?

☐ Condition? ______________

WINDOWS

☐ Condition? ______________

CEILING

☐ Condition? ______________

ROOMS

Y N

☐☐ Natural Lighting?

☐☐ Even Floors?

☐☐ Smoke Detectors?

☐☐ Carbon Monoxide Detector?

WALLS

Y N

☐☐ Stains?

☐☐ Need Re-painting?

☐☐ Soundproof?

STAIRS

Y N

☐☐ Creaky?

☐☐ Signs of Damage?

DOORS

Y N

☐☐ Open & Close Property

☐☐ Weather Proofed

☐☐ Working Doorbell

BATHROOM

Y N

☐☐ Stain-free?

☐☐ Mildew/Mold-free?

☐☐ Leak-free?

☐☐ Cabinet & Storage Space?

☐☐ Working Fans?

☐☐ Functioning Toilet?

KITCHEN

Y N

☐☐ Stain-free?

☐☐ Mildew/Mold-free?

☐☐ Leak-free?

☐☐ Cabinet & Storage Space?

☐☐ Working Fans?

☐☐ Working Garbage Disposal?

EXTERIOR

UP-TO-DATE SYSTEMS

☐ Hire Home Inspector [*before purchase*]

☐ Electrical

☐ A/C

☐ Heating

☐ Security

☐ Plumbing

☐ Water

☐ Sewer Insulation

ROOF

Y N

☐☐ Sagging Roof Line?

☐☐ Discoloration?

☐☐ Holes?

FOUNDATION, DRIVEWAY, & POOL

FOUNDATION

☐ Visible Cracks? ___________

DRIVEWAY

☐ Visible Cracks? ___________

POOL

☐ Visible Cracks? ___________

☐ Above Ground? ___________

GARAGE

Y N

☐☐ Functional - Manual?

☐☐ Functional - Remote?

☐ N/A

SIDING

Y N

☐☐ Paint Peeling?

☐☐ Cracks/Splits?

LANDSCAPING & CURB APPEAL

☐ Trees - Condition?

____

☐ Lawn [*front*] - Condition?

____

☐ Lawn [*back*] - Condition?

____

☐ Fences - Condition?

____

☐ Landscaping - Condition?

____

15

PROPERTY INFORMATION

ADDRESS	

BEDROOMS		BATHROOMS		Sq. Ft.	
LOT SIZE		YEAR BUILT		SCHOOL DISTRICT	
ANNUAL TAX		PRICE			

REALTOR INFORMATION

NAME	
AGENCY	
PHONE	
EMAIL	

NOTES AND REMINDERS

INSPECTION CHECKLIST

INTERIOR

FLOORING, WINDOWS & CEILING

FLOOR
- ☐ Age?
- ☐ Condition? ____________

WINDOWS
- ☐ Condition? ____________

CEILING
- ☐ Condition? ____________

ROOMS

Y N
- ☐☐ Natural Lighting?
- ☐☐ Even Floors?
- ☐☐ Smoke Detectors?
- ☐☐ Carbon Monoxide Detector?

WALLS

Y N
- ☐☐ Stains?
- ☐☐ Need Re-painting?
- ☐☐ Soundproof?

STAIRS

Y N
- ☐☐ Creaky?
- ☐☐ Signs of Damage?

DOORS

Y N
- ☐☐ Open & Close Property
- ☐☐ Weather Proofed
- ☐☐ Working Doorbell

BATHROOM

Y N
- ☐☐ Stain-free?
- ☐☐ Mildew/Mold-free?
- ☐☐ Leak-free?
- ☐☐ Cabinet & Storage Space?
- ☐☐ Working Fans?
- ☐☐ Functioning Toilet?

KITCHEN

Y N
- ☐☐ Stain-free?
- ☐☐ Mildew/Mold-free?
- ☐☐ Leak-free?
- ☐☐ Cabinet & Storage Space?
- ☐☐ Working Fans?
- ☐☐ Working Garbage Disposal?

EXTERIOR

UP-TO-DATE SYSTEMS

- ☐ Hire Home Inspector [*before purchase*]
- ☐ Electrical
- ☐ A/C
- ☐ Heating
- ☐ Security
- ☐ Plumbing
- ☐ Water
- ☐ Sewer Insulation

ROOF

Y N
- ☐☐ Sagging Roof Line?
- ☐☐ Discoloration?
- ☐☐ Holes?

FOUNDATION, DRIVEWAY, & POOL

FOUNDATION
- ☐ Visible Cracks? __________

DRIVEWAY
- ☐ Visible Cracks? __________

POOL
- ☐ Visible Cracks? __________
- ☐ Above Ground? __________

GARAGE

Y N
- ☐☐ Functional - Manual?
- ☐☐ Functional - Remote?
- ☐ N/A

SIDING

Y N
- ☐☐ Paint Peeling?
- ☐☐ Cracks/Splits?

LANDSCAPING & CURB APPEAL

- ☐ Trees - Condition?
  ____
- ☐ Lawn [*front*] - Condition?
  ____
- ☐ Lawn [*back*] - Condition?
  ____
- ☐ Fences - Condition?
  ____
- ☐ Landscaping - Condition?
  ____

16

PROPERTY INFORMATION

ADDRESS					
BEDROOMS		**BATHROOMS**		**Sq. Ft.**	
LOT SIZE		**YEAR BUILT**		**SCHOOL DISTRICT**	
ANNUAL TAX			**PRICE**		

REALTOR INFORMATION

NAME	
AGENCY	
PHONE	
EMAIL	

NOTES AND REMINDERS

INSPECTION CHECKLIST

INTERIOR

FLOORING, WINDOWS & CEILING

FLOOR

☐ Age?

☐ Condition? _____________

WINDOWS

☐ Condition? _____________

CEILING

☐ Condition? _____________

ROOMS

Y N

☐☐ Natural Lighting?

☐☐ Even Floors?

☐☐ Smoke Detectors?

☐☐ Carbon Monoxide Detector?

WALLS

Y N

☐☐ Stains?

☐☐ Need Re-painting?

☐☐ Soundproof?

STAIRS

Y N

☐☐ Creaky?

☐☐ Signs of Damage?

DOORS

Y N

☐☐ Open & Close Property

☐☐ Weather Proofed

☐☐ Working Doorbell

BATHROOM

Y N

☐☐ Stain-free?

☐☐ Mildew/Mold-free?

☐☐ Leak-free?

☐☐ Cabinet & Storage Space?

☐☐ Working Fans?

☐☐ Functioning Toilet?

KITCHEN

Y N

☐☐ Stain-free?

☐☐ Mildew/Mold-free?

☐☐ Leak-free?

☐☐ Cabinet & Storage Space?

☐☐ Working Fans?

☐☐ Working Garbage Disposal?

EXTERIOR

UP-TO-DATE SYSTEMS

☐ Hire Home Inspector [*before purchase*]

☐ Electrical

☐ A/C

☐ Heating

☐ Security

☐ Plumbing

☐ Water

☐ Sewer Insulation

ROOF

Y N

☐☐ Sagging Roof Line?

☐☐ Discoloration?

☐☐ Holes?

FOUNDATION, DRIVEWAY, & POOL

FOUNDATION

☐ Visible Cracks? _____________

DRIVEWAY

☐ Visible Cracks? _____________

POOL

☐ Visible Cracks? _____________

☐ Above Ground? _____________

GARAGE

Y N

☐☐ Functional - Manual?

☐☐ Functional - Remote?

☐ N/A

SIDING

Y N

☐☐ Paint Peeling?

☐☐ Cracks/Splits?

LANDSCAPING & CURB APPEAL

☐ Trees - Condition?

____

☐ Lawn [*front*] - Condition?

____

☐ Lawn [*back*] - Condition?

____

☐ Fences - Condition?

____

☐ Landscaping - Condition?

____

17

PROPERTY INFORMATION

ADDRESS					
BEDROOMS		BATHROOMS		Sq. Ft.	
LOT SIZE		YEAR BUILT		SCHOOL DISTRICT	
ANNUAL TAX		PRICE			

REALTOR INFORMATION

NAME	
AGENCY	
PHONE	
EMAIL	

NOTES AND REMINDERS

INSPECTION CHECKLIST

INTERIOR

FLOORING, WINDOWS & CEILING

FLOOR

☐ Age?

☐ Condition? _______________

WINDOWS

☐ Condition? _______________

CEILING

☐ Condition? _______________

ROOMS

Y N

☐☐ Natural Lighting?

☐☐ Even Floors?

☐☐ Smoke Detectors?

☐☐ Carbon Monoxide Detector?

WALLS

Y N

☐☐ Stains?

☐☐ Need Re-painting?

☐☐ Soundproof?

STAIRS

Y N

☐☐ Creaky?

☐☐ Signs of Damage?

DOORS

Y N

☐☐ Open & Close Property

☐☐ Weather Proofed

☐☐ Working Doorbell

BATHROOM

Y N

☐☐ Stain-free?

☐☐ Mildew/Mold-free?

☐☐ Leak-free?

☐☐ Cabinet & Storage Space?

☐☐ Working Fans?

☐☐ Functioning Toilet?

KITCHEN

Y N

☐☐ Stain-free?

☐☐ Mildew/Mold-free?

☐☐ Leak-free?

☐☐ Cabinet & Storage Space?

☐☐ Working Fans?

☐☐ Working Garbage Disposal?

EXTERIOR

UP-TO-DATE SYSTEMS

☐ Hire Home Inspector [*before purchase*]

☐ Electrical

☐ A/C

☐ Heating

☐ Security

☐ Plumbing

☐ Water

☐ Sewer Insulation

ROOF

Y N

☐☐ Sagging Roof Line?

☐☐ Discoloration?

☐☐ Holes?

FOUNDATION, DRIVEWAY, & POOL

FOUNDATION

☐ Visible Cracks? _______________

DRIVEWAY

☐ Visible Cracks? _______________

POOL

☐ Visible Cracks? _______________

☐ Above Ground? _______________

GARAGE

Y N

☐☐ Functional - Manual?

☐☐ Functional - Remote?

☐ N/A

SIDING

Y N

☐☐ Paint Peeling?

☐☐ Cracks/Splits?

LANDSCAPING & CURB APPEAL

☐ Trees - Condition?

____

☐ Lawn [*front*] - Condition?

____

☐ Lawn [*back*] - Condition?

____

☐ Fences - Condition?

____

☐ Landscaping - Condition?

____

18

PROPERTY INFORMATION

ADDRESS	
BEDROOMS		BATHROOMS		Sq. Ft.	
LOT SIZE		YEAR BUILT		SCHOOL DISTRICT	
ANNUAL TAX		PRICE	

REALTOR INFORMATION

NAME	
AGENCY	
PHONE	
EMAIL	

NOTES AND REMINDERS

INSPECTION CHECKLIST

INTERIOR

FLOORING, WINDOWS & CEILING

FLOOR
- ☐ Age?
- ☐ Condition? _______________

WINDOWS
- ☐ Condition? _______________

CEILING
- ☐ Condition? _______________

ROOMS

Y N
- ☐☐ Natural Lighting?
- ☐☐ Even Floors?
- ☐☐ Smoke Detectors?
- ☐☐ Carbon Monoxide Detector?

WALLS

Y N
- ☐☐ Stains?
- ☐☐ Need Re-painting?
- ☐☐ Soundproof?

STAIRS

Y N
- ☐☐ Creaky?
- ☐☐ Signs of Damage?

DOORS

Y N
- ☐☐ Open & Close Property
- ☐☐ Weather Proofed
- ☐☐ Working Doorbell

BATHROOM

Y N
- ☐☐ Stain-free?
- ☐☐ Mildew/Mold-free?
- ☐☐ Leak-free?
- ☐☐ Cabinet & Storage Space?
- ☐☐ Working Fans?
- ☐☐ Functioning Toilet?

KITCHEN

Y N
- ☐☐ Stain-free?
- ☐☐ Mildew/Mold-free?
- ☐☐ Leak-free?
- ☐☐ Cabinet & Storage Space?
- ☐☐ Working Fans?
- ☐☐ Working Garbage Disposal?

EXTERIOR

UP-TO-DATE SYSTEMS

- ☐ Hire Home Inspector [*before purchase*]
- ☐ Electrical
- ☐ A/C
- ☐ Heating
- ☐ Security
- ☐ Plumbing
- ☐ Water
- ☐ Sewer Insulation

ROOF

Y N
- ☐☐ Sagging Roof Line?
- ☐☐ Discoloration?
- ☐☐ Holes?

FOUNDATION, DRIVEWAY, & POOL

FOUNDATION
- ☐ Visible Cracks? _______________

DRIVEWAY
- ☐ Visible Cracks? _______________

POOL
- ☐ Visible Cracks? _______________
- ☐ Above Ground? _______________

GARAGE

Y N
- ☐☐ Functional - Manual?
- ☐☐ Functional - Remote?
- ☐ N/A

SIDING

Y N
- ☐☐ Paint Peeling?
- ☐☐ Cracks/Splits?

LANDSCAPING & CURB APPEAL

- ☐ Trees - Condition?
  ____

- ☐ Lawn [*front*] - Condition?
  ____

- ☐ Lawn [*back*] - Condition?
  ____

- ☐ Fences - Condition?
  ____

- ☐ Landscaping - Condition?
  ____

19

PROPERTY INFORMATION

ADDRESS	

BEDROOMS		BATHROOMS		Sq. Ft.	
LOT SIZE		YEAR BUILT		SCHOOL DISTRICT	
ANNUAL TAX		PRICE			

REALTOR INFORMATION

NAME	
AGENCY	
PHONE	
EMAIL	

NOTES AND REMINDERS

INSPECTION CHECKLIST

INTERIOR

FLOORING, WINDOWS & CEILING

FLOOR

- ☐ Age?
- ☐ Condition? ______________

WINDOWS

- ☐ Condition? ______________

CEILING

- ☐ Condition? ______________

ROOMS

Y N

- ☐☐ Natural Lighting?
- ☐☐ Even Floors?
- ☐☐ Smoke Detectors?
- ☐☐ Carbon Monoxide Detector?

WALLS

Y N

- ☐☐ Stains?
- ☐☐ Need Re-painting?
- ☐☐ Soundproof?

STAIRS

Y N

- ☐☐ Creaky?
- ☐☐ Signs of Damage?

DOORS

Y N

- ☐☐ Open & Close Property
- ☐☐ Weather Proofed
- ☐☐ Working Doorbell

BATHROOM

Y N

- ☐☐ Stain-free?
- ☐☐ Mildew/Mold-free?
- ☐☐ Leak-free?
- ☐☐ Cabinet & Storage Space?
- ☐☐ Working Fans?
- ☐☐ Functioning Toilet?

KITCHEN

Y N

- ☐☐ Stain-free?
- ☐☐ Mildew/Mold-free?
- ☐☐ Leak-free?
- ☐☐ Cabinet & Storage Space?
- ☐☐ Working Fans?
- ☐☐ Working Garbage Disposal?

EXTERIOR

UP-TO-DATE SYSTEMS

- ☐ Hire Home Inspector [*before purchase*]
- ☐ Electrical
- ☐ A/C
- ☐ Heating
- ☐ Security
- ☐ Plumbing
- ☐ Water
- ☐ Sewer Insulation

ROOF

Y N

- ☐☐ Sagging Roof Line?
- ☐☐ Discoloration?
- ☐☐ Holes?

FOUNDATION, DRIVEWAY, & POOL

FOUNDATION

- ☐ Visible Cracks? ___________

DRIVEWAY

- ☐ Visible Cracks? ___________

POOL

- ☐ Visible Cracks? ___________
- ☐ Above Ground? ___________

GARAGE

Y N

- ☐☐ Functional - Manual?
- ☐☐ Functional - Remote?
- ☐ N/A

SIDING

Y N

- ☐☐ Paint Peeling?
- ☐☐ Cracks/Splits?

LANDSCAPING & CURB APPEAL

- ☐ Trees - Condition?

  ____

- ☐ Lawn [*front*] - Condition?

  ____

- ☐ Lawn [*back*] - Condition?

  ____

- ☐ Fences - Condition?

  ____

- ☐ Landscaping - Condition?

  ____

20

PROPERTY INFORMATION

ADDRESS	

BEDROOMS		BATHROOMS		Sq. Ft.	
LOT SIZE		YEAR BUILT		SCHOOL DISTRICT	
ANNUAL TAX		PRICE			

REALTOR INFORMATION

NAME	
AGENCY	
PHONE	
EMAIL	

NOTES AND REMINDERS

INSPECTION CHECKLIST

INTERIOR

FLOORING, WINDOWS & CEILING

FLOOR

☐ Age?

☐ Condition? ____________

WINDOWS

☐ Condition? ____________

CEILING

☐ Condition? ____________

ROOMS

Y N

☐☐ Natural Lighting?

☐☐ Even Floors?

☐☐ Smoke Detectors?

☐☐ Carbon Monoxide Detector?

WALLS

Y N

☐☐ Stains?

☐☐ Need Re-painting?

☐☐ Soundproof?

STAIRS

Y N

☐☐ Creaky?

☐☐ Signs of Damage?

DOORS

Y N

☐☐ Open & Close Property

☐☐ Weather Proofed

☐☐ Working Doorbell

BATHROOM

Y N

☐☐ Stain-free?

☐☐ Mildew/Mold-free?

☐☐ Leak-free?

☐☐ Cabinet & Storage Space?

☐☐ Working Fans?

☐☐ Functioning Toilet?

KITCHEN

Y N

☐☐ Stain-free?

☐☐ Mildew/Mold-free?

☐☐ Leak-free?

☐☐ Cabinet & Storage Space?

☐☐ Working Fans?

☐☐ Working Garbage Disposal?

EXTERIOR

UP-TO-DATE SYSTEMS

☐ Hire Home Inspector [*before purchase*]

☐ Electrical

☐ A/C

☐ Heating

☐ Security

☐ Plumbing

☐ Water

☐ Sewer Insulation

ROOF

Y N

☐☐ Sagging Roof Line?

☐☐ Discoloration?

☐☐ Holes?

FOUNDATION, DRIVEWAY, & POOL

FOUNDATION

☐ Visible Cracks? __________

DRIVEWAY

☐ Visible Cracks? __________

POOL

☐ Visible Cracks? __________

☐ Above Ground? __________

GARAGE

Y N

☐☐ Functional - Manual?

☐☐ Functional - Remote?

☐ N/A

SIDING

Y N

☐☐ Paint Peeling?

☐☐ Cracks/Splits?

LANDSCAPING & CURB APPEAL

☐ Trees - Condition?

____

☐ Lawn [*front*] - Condition?

____

☐ Lawn [*back*] - Condition?

____

☐ Fences - Condition?

____

☐ Landscaping - Condition?

____

21

PROPERTY INFORMATION

ADDRESS	

BEDROOMS		**BATHROOMS**		**Sq. Ft.**	
LOT SIZE		**YEAR BUILT**		**SCHOOL DISTRICT**	
ANNUAL TAX		**PRICE**			

REALTOR INFORMATION

NAME	
AGENCY	
PHONE	
EMAIL	

NOTES AND REMINDERS

INSPECTION CHECKLIST

INTERIOR

FLOORING, WINDOWS & CEILING

FLOOR

- ☐ Age?
- ☐ Condition? _____________

WINDOWS

- ☐ Condition? _____________

CEILING

- ☐ Condition? _____________

ROOMS

Y N

- ☐☐ Natural Lighting?
- ☐☐ Even Floors?
- ☐☐ Smoke Detectors?
- ☐☐ Carbon Monoxide Detector?

WALLS

Y N

- ☐☐ Stains?
- ☐☐ Need Re-painting?
- ☐☐ Soundproof?

STAIRS

Y N

- ☐☐ Creaky?
- ☐☐ Signs of Damage?

DOORS

Y N

- ☐☐ Open & Close Property
- ☐☐ Weather Proofed
- ☐☐ Working Doorbell

BATHROOM

Y N

- ☐☐ Stain-free?
- ☐☐ Mildew/Mold-free?
- ☐☐ Leak-free?
- ☐☐ Cabinet & Storage Space?
- ☐☐ Working Fans?
- ☐☐ Functioning Toilet?

KITCHEN

Y N

- ☐☐ Stain-free?
- ☐☐ Mildew/Mold-free?
- ☐☐ Leak-free?
- ☐☐ Cabinet & Storage Space?
- ☐☐ Working Fans?
- ☐☐ Working Garbage Disposal?

EXTERIOR

UP-TO-DATE SYSTEMS

- ☐ Hire Home Inspector [*before purchase*]
- ☐ Electrical
- ☐ A/C
- ☐ Heating
- ☐ Security
- ☐ Plumbing
- ☐ Water
- ☐ Sewer Insulation

ROOF

Y N

- ☐☐ Sagging Roof Line?
- ☐☐ Discoloration?
- ☐☐ Holes?

FOUNDATION, DRIVEWAY, & POOL

FOUNDATION

- ☐ Visible Cracks? _____________

DRIVEWAY

- ☐ Visible Cracks? _____________

POOL

- ☐ Visible Cracks? _____________
- ☐ Above Ground? _____________

GARAGE

Y N

- ☐☐ Functional - Manual?
- ☐☐ Functional - Remote?
- ☐ N/A

SIDING

Y N

- ☐☐ Paint Peeling?
- ☐☐ Cracks/Splits?

LANDSCAPING & CURB APPEAL

- ☐ Trees - Condition?

____

- ☐ Lawn [*front*] - Condition?

____

- ☐ Lawn [*back*] - Condition?

____

- ☐ Fences - Condition?

____

- ☐ Landscaping - Condition?

____

PROPERTY INFORMATION

ADDRESS	
BEDROOMS		BATHROOMS		Sq. Ft.	
LOT SIZE		YEAR BUILT		SCHOOL DISTRICT	
ANNUAL TAX		PRICE	

REALTOR INFORMATION

NAME	
AGENCY	
PHONE	
EMAIL	

NOTES AND REMINDERS

INSPECTION CHECKLIST

INTERIOR

FLOORING, WINDOWS & CEILING

FLOOR

- ☐ Age?
- ☐ Condition? ___________

WINDOWS

- ☐ Condition? ___________

CEILING

- ☐ Condition? ___________

ROOMS

Y N

- ☐☐ Natural Lighting?
- ☐☐ Even Floors?
- ☐☐ Smoke Detectors?
- ☐☐ Carbon Monoxide Detector?

WALLS

Y N

- ☐☐ Stains?
- ☐☐ Need Re-painting?
- ☐☐ Soundproof?

STAIRS

Y N

- ☐☐ Creaky?
- ☐☐ Signs of Damage?

DOORS

Y N

- ☐☐ Open & Close Property
- ☐☐ Weather Proofed
- ☐☐ Working Doorbell

BATHROOM

Y N

- ☐☐ Stain-free?
- ☐☐ Mildew/Mold-free?
- ☐☐ Leak-free?
- ☐☐ Cabinet & Storage Space?
- ☐☐ Working Fans?
- ☐☐ Functioning Toilet?

KITCHEN

Y N

- ☐☐ Stain-free?
- ☐☐ Mildew/Mold-free?
- ☐☐ Leak-free?
- ☐☐ Cabinet & Storage Space?
- ☐☐ Working Fans?
- ☐☐ Working Garbage Disposal?

EXTERIOR

UP-TO-DATE SYSTEMS

- ☐ Hire Home Inspector [*before purchase*]
- ☐ Electrical
- ☐ A/C
- ☐ Heating
- ☐ Security
- ☐ Plumbing
- ☐ Water
- ☐ Sewer Insulation

ROOF

Y N

- ☐☐ Sagging Roof Line?
- ☐☐ Discoloration?
- ☐☐ Holes?

FOUNDATION, DRIVEWAY, & POOL

FOUNDATION

- ☐ Visible Cracks? ___________

DRIVEWAY

- ☐ Visible Cracks? ___________

POOL

- ☐ Visible Cracks? ___________
- ☐ Above Ground? ___________

GARAGE

Y N

- ☐☐ Functional - Manual?
- ☐☐ Functional - Remote?
- ☐ N/A

SIDING

Y N

- ☐☐ Paint Peeling?
- ☐☐ Cracks/Splits?

LANDSCAPING & CURB APPEAL

- ☐ Trees - Condition?

  ____

- ☐ Lawn [*front*] - Condition?

  ____

- ☐ Lawn [*back*] - Condition?

  ____

- ☐ Fences - Condition?

  ____

- ☐ Landscaping - Condition?

  ____

23

PROPERTY INFORMATION

ADDRESS					
BEDROOMS		BATHROOMS		Sq. Ft.	
LOT SIZE		YEAR BUILT		SCHOOL DISTRICT	
ANNUAL TAX		PRICE			

REALTOR INFORMATION

NAME	
AGENCY	
PHONE	
EMAIL	

NOTES AND REMINDERS

INSPECTION CHECKLIST

INTERIOR

FLOORING, WINDOWS & CEILING

FLOOR

- ☐ Age?
- ☐ Condition? ______________

WINDOWS

- ☐ Condition? ______________

CEILING

- ☐ Condition? ______________

ROOMS

Y N

- ☐☐ Natural Lighting?
- ☐☐ Even Floors?
- ☐☐ Smoke Detectors?
- ☐☐ Carbon Monoxide Detector?

WALLS

Y N

- ☐☐ Stains?
- ☐☐ Need Re-painting?
- ☐☐ Soundproof?

STAIRS

Y N

- ☐☐ Creaky?
- ☐☐ Signs of Damage?

DOORS

Y N

- ☐☐ Open & Close Property
- ☐☐ Weather Proofed
- ☐☐ Working Doorbell

BATHROOM

Y N

- ☐☐ Stain-free?
- ☐☐ Mildew/Mold-free?
- ☐☐ Leak-free?
- ☐☐ Cabinet & Storage Space?
- ☐☐ Working Fans?
- ☐☐ Functioning Toilet?

KITCHEN

Y N

- ☐☐ Stain-free?
- ☐☐ Mildew/Mold-free?
- ☐☐ Leak-free?
- ☐☐ Cabinet & Storage Space?
- ☐☐ Working Fans?
- ☐☐ Working Garbage Disposal?

EXTERIOR

UP-TO-DATE SYSTEMS

- ☐ Hire Home Inspector [*before purchase*]
- ☐ Electrical
- ☐ A/C
- ☐ Heating
- ☐ Security
- ☐ Plumbing
- ☐ Water
- ☐ Sewer Insulation

ROOF

Y N

- ☐☐ Sagging Roof Line?
- ☐☐ Discoloration?
- ☐☐ Holes?

FOUNDATION, DRIVEWAY, & POOL

FOUNDATION

- ☐ Visible Cracks? ___________

DRIVEWAY

- ☐ Visible Cracks? ___________

POOL

- ☐ Visible Cracks? ___________
- ☐ Above Ground? ___________

GARAGE

Y N

- ☐☐ Functional - Manual?
- ☐☐ Functional - Remote?
- ☐ N/A

SIDING

Y N

- ☐☐ Paint Peeling?
- ☐☐ Cracks/Splits?

LANDSCAPING & CURB APPEAL

- ☐ Trees - Condition?

  ____

- ☐ Lawn [*front*] - Condition?

  ____

- ☐ Lawn [*back*] - Condition?

  ____

- ☐ Fences - Condition?

  ____

- ☐ Landscaping - Condition?

  ____

24

PROPERTY INFORMATION

ADDRESS						
BEDROOMS		BATHROOMS		Sq. Ft.		
LOT SIZE		YEAR BUILT		SCHOOL DISTRICT		
ANNUAL TAX			PRICE			

REALTOR INFORMATION

NAME	
AGENCY	
PHONE	
EMAIL	

NOTES AND REMINDERS

INSPECTION CHECKLIST

INTERIOR

FLOORING, WINDOWS & CEILING

FLOOR
- ☐ Age?
- ☐ Condition? ______________

WINDOWS
- ☐ Condition? ______________

CEILING
- ☐ Condition? ______________

ROOMS

Y N
- ☐☐ Natural Lighting?
- ☐☐ Even Floors?
- ☐☐ Smoke Detectors?
- ☐☐ Carbon Monoxide Detector?

WALLS

Y N
- ☐☐ Stains?
- ☐☐ Need Re-painting?
- ☐☐ Soundproof?

STAIRS

Y N
- ☐☐ Creaky?
- ☐☐ Signs of Damage?

DOORS

Y N
- ☐☐ Open & Close Property
- ☐☐ Weather Proofed
- ☐☐ Working Doorbell

BATHROOM

Y N
- ☐☐ Stain-free?
- ☐☐ Mildew/Mold-free?
- ☐☐ Leak-free?
- ☐☐ Cabinet & Storage Space?
- ☐☐ Working Fans?
- ☐☐ Functioning Toilet?

KITCHEN

Y N
- ☐☐ Stain-free?
- ☐☐ Mildew/Mold-free?
- ☐☐ Leak-free?
- ☐☐ Cabinet & Storage Space?
- ☐☐ Working Fans?
- ☐☐ Working Garbage Disposal?

EXTERIOR

UP-TO-DATE SYSTEMS

- ☐ Hire Home Inspector [*before purchase*]
- ☐ Electrical
- ☐ A/C
- ☐ Heating
- ☐ Security
- ☐ Plumbing
- ☐ Water
- ☐ Sewer Insulation

ROOF

Y N
- ☐☐ Sagging Roof Line?
- ☐☐ Discoloration?
- ☐☐ Holes?

FOUNDATION, DRIVEWAY, & POOL

FOUNDATION
- ☐ Visible Cracks? ___________

DRIVEWAY
- ☐ Visible Cracks? ___________

POOL
- ☐ Visible Cracks? ___________
- ☐ Above Ground? ___________

GARAGE

Y N
- ☐☐ Functional - Manual?
- ☐☐ Functional - Remote?
- ☐ N/A

SIDING

Y N
- ☐☐ Paint Peeling?
- ☐☐ Cracks/Splits?

LANDSCAPING & CURB APPEAL

- ☐ Trees - Condition?

  ____

- ☐ Lawn [*front*] - Condition?

  ____

- ☐ Lawn [*back*] - Condition?

  ____

- ☐ Fences - Condition?

  ____

- ☐ Landscaping - Condition?

  ____

PROPERTY INFORMATION

ADDRESS	
BEDROOMS		BATHROOMS		Sq. Ft.	
LOT SIZE		YEAR BUILT		SCHOOL DISTRICT	
ANNUAL TAX		PRICE	

REALTOR INFORMATION

NAME	
AGENCY	
PHONE	
EMAIL	

NOTES AND REMINDERS

INSPECTION CHECKLIST

INTERIOR

FLOORING, WINDOWS & CEILING

FLOOR

- ☐ Age?
- ☐ Condition? ___________

WINDOWS

- ☐ Condition? ___________

CEILING

- ☐ Condition? ___________

ROOMS

Y N

- ☐☐ Natural Lighting?
- ☐☐ Even Floors?
- ☐☐ Smoke Detectors?
- ☐☐ Carbon Monoxide Detector?

WALLS

Y N

- ☐☐ Stains?
- ☐☐ Need Re-painting?
- ☐☐ Soundproof?

STAIRS

Y N

- ☐☐ Creaky?
- ☐☐ Signs of Damage?

DOORS

Y N

- ☐☐ Open & Close Property
- ☐☐ Weather Proofed
- ☐☐ Working Doorbell

BATHROOM

Y N

- ☐☐ Stain-free?
- ☐☐ Mildew/Mold-free?
- ☐☐ Leak-free?
- ☐☐ Cabinet & Storage Space?
- ☐☐ Working Fans?
- ☐☐ Functioning Toilet?

KITCHEN

Y N

- ☐☐ Stain-free?
- ☐☐ Mildew/Mold-free?
- ☐☐ Leak-free?
- ☐☐ Cabinet & Storage Space?
- ☐☐ Working Fans?
- ☐☐ Working Garbage Disposal?

EXTERIOR

UP-TO-DATE SYSTEMS

- ☐ Hire Home Inspector [*before purchase*]
- ☐ Electrical
- ☐ A/C
- ☐ Heating
- ☐ Security
- ☐ Plumbing
- ☐ Water
- ☐ Sewer Insulation

ROOF

Y N

- ☐☐ Sagging Roof Line?
- ☐☐ Discoloration?
- ☐☐ Holes?

FOUNDATION, DRIVEWAY, & POOL

FOUNDATION

- ☐ Visible Cracks? ___________

DRIVEWAY

- ☐ Visible Cracks? ___________

POOL

- ☐ Visible Cracks? ___________
- ☐ Above Ground? ___________

GARAGE

Y N

- ☐☐ Functional - Manual?
- ☐☐ Functional - Remote?
- ☐ N/A

SIDING

Y N

- ☐☐ Paint Peeling?
- ☐☐ Cracks/Splits?

LANDSCAPING & CURB APPEAL

- ☐ Trees - Condition?

  ____

- ☐ Lawn [*front*] - Condition?

  ____

- ☐ Lawn [*back*] - Condition?

  ____

- ☐ Fences - Condition?

  ____

- ☐ Landscaping - Condition?

  ____

26

PROPERTY INFORMATION

ADDRESS	
BEDROOMS		BATHROOMS		Sq. Ft.	
LOT SIZE		YEAR BUILT		SCHOOL DISTRICT	
ANNUAL TAX		PRICE	

REALTOR INFORMATION

NAME	
AGENCY	
PHONE	
EMAIL	

NOTES AND REMINDERS

INSPECTION CHECKLIST

INTERIOR

FLOORING, WINDOWS & CEILING

FLOOR

☐ Age?

☐ Condition? _______________

WINDOWS

☐ Condition? _______________

CEILING

☐ Condition? _______________

ROOMS

Y N

☐☐ Natural Lighting?

☐☐ Even Floors?

☐☐ Smoke Detectors?

☐☐ Carbon Monoxide Detector?

WALLS

Y N

☐☐ Stains?

☐☐ Need Re-painting?

☐☐ Soundproof?

STAIRS

Y N

☐☐ Creaky?

☐☐ Signs of Damage?

DOORS

Y N

☐☐ Open & Close Property

☐☐ Weather Proofed

☐☐ Working Doorbell

BATHROOM

Y N

☐☐ Stain-free?

☐☐ Mildew/Mold-free?

☐☐ Leak-free?

☐☐ Cabinet & Storage Space?

☐☐ Working Fans?

☐☐ Functioning Toilet?

KITCHEN

Y N

☐☐ Stain-free?

☐☐ Mildew/Mold-free?

☐☐ Leak-free?

☐☐ Cabinet & Storage Space?

☐☐ Working Fans?

☐☐ Working Garbage Disposal?

EXTERIOR

UP-TO-DATE SYSTEMS

☐ Hire Home Inspector [*before purchase*]

☐ Electrical

☐ A/C

☐ Heating

☐ Security

☐ Plumbing

☐ Water

☐ Sewer Insulation

ROOF

Y N

☐☐ Sagging Roof Line?

☐☐ Discoloration?

☐☐ Holes?

FOUNDATION, DRIVEWAY, & POOL

FOUNDATION

☐ Visible Cracks? _______________

DRIVEWAY

☐ Visible Cracks? _______________

POOL

☐ Visible Cracks? _______________

☐ Above Ground? _______________

GARAGE

Y N

☐☐ Functional - Manual?

☐☐ Functional - Remote?

☐ N/A

SIDING

Y N

☐☐ Paint Peeling?

☐☐ Cracks/Splits?

LANDSCAPING & CURB APPEAL

☐ Trees - Condition?

____

☐ Lawn [*front*] - Condition?

____

☐ Lawn [*back*] - Condition?

____

☐ Fences - Condition?

____

☐ Landscaping - Condition?

____

27

PROPERTY INFORMATION

ADDRESS					
BEDROOMS		**BATHROOMS**		**Sq. Ft.**	
LOT SIZE		**YEAR BUILT**		**SCHOOL DISTRICT**	
ANNUAL TAX		**PRICE**			

REALTOR INFORMATION

NAME	
AGENCY	
PHONE	
EMAIL	

NOTES AND REMINDERS

INSPECTION CHECKLIST

INTERIOR

FLOORING, WINDOWS & CEILING

FLOOR

☐ Age?

☐ Condition? _____________

WINDOWS

☐ Condition? _____________

CEILING

☐ Condition? _____________

ROOMS

Y N

☐☐ Natural Lighting?

☐☐ Even Floors?

☐☐ Smoke Detectors?

☐☐ Carbon Monoxide Detector?

WALLS

Y N

☐☐ Stains?

☐☐ Need Re-painting?

☐☐ Soundproof?

STAIRS

Y N

☐☐ Creaky?

☐☐ Signs of Damage?

DOORS

Y N

☐☐ Open & Close Property

☐☐ Weather Proofed

☐☐ Working Doorbell

BATHROOM

Y N

☐☐ Stain-free?

☐☐ Mildew/Mold-free?

☐☐ Leak-free?

☐☐ Cabinet & Storage Space?

☐☐ Working Fans?

☐☐ Functioning Toilet?

KITCHEN

Y N

☐☐ Stain-free?

☐☐ Mildew/Mold-free?

☐☐ Leak-free?

☐☐ Cabinet & Storage Space?

☐☐ Working Fans?

☐☐ Working Garbage Disposal?

EXTERIOR

UP-TO-DATE SYSTEMS

☐ Hire Home Inspector [*before purchase*]

☐ Electrical

☐ A/C

☐ Heating

☐ Security

☐ Plumbing

☐ Water

☐ Sewer Insulation

ROOF

Y N

☐☐ Sagging Roof Line?

☐☐ Discoloration?

☐☐ Holes?

FOUNDATION, DRIVEWAY, & POOL

FOUNDATION

☐ Visible Cracks? _____________

DRIVEWAY

☐ Visible Cracks? _____________

POOL

☐ Visible Cracks? _____________

☐ Above Ground? _____________

GARAGE

Y N

☐☐ Functional - Manual?

☐☐ Functional - Remote?

☐ N/A

SIDING

Y N

☐☐ Paint Peeling?

☐☐ Cracks/Splits?

LANDSCAPING & CURB APPEAL

☐ Trees - Condition?

____

☐ Lawn [*front*] - Condition?

____

☐ Lawn [*back*] - Condition?

____

☐ Fences - Condition?

____

☐ Landscaping - Condition?

____

28

PROPERTY INFORMATION

ADDRESS	
BEDROOMS		BATHROOMS		Sq. Ft.	
LOT SIZE		YEAR BUILT		SCHOOL DISTRICT	
ANNUAL TAX		**PRICE**	

REALTOR INFORMATION

NAME	
AGENCY	
PHONE	
EMAIL	

NOTES AND REMINDERS

INSPECTION CHECKLIST

INTERIOR

FLOORING, WINDOWS & CEILING

FLOOR

☐ Age?

☐ Condition? _____________

WINDOWS

☐ Condition? _____________

CEILING

☐ Condition? _____________

ROOMS

Y N

☐☐ Natural Lighting?

☐☐ Even Floors?

☐☐ Smoke Detectors?

☐☐ Carbon Monoxide Detector?

WALLS

Y N

☐☐ Stains?

☐☐ Need Re-painting?

☐☐ Soundproof?

STAIRS

Y N

☐☐ Creaky?

☐☐ Signs of Damage?

DOORS

Y N

☐☐ Open & Close Property

☐☐ Weather Proofed

☐☐ Working Doorbell

BATHROOM

Y N

☐☐ Stain-free?

☐☐ Mildew/Mold-free?

☐☐ Leak-free?

☐☐ Cabinet & Storage Space?

☐☐ Working Fans?

☐☐ Functioning Toilet?

KITCHEN

Y N

☐☐ Stain-free?

☐☐ Mildew/Mold-free?

☐☐ Leak-free?

☐☐ Cabinet & Storage Space?

☐☐ Working Fans?

☐☐ Working Garbage Disposal?

EXTERIOR

UP-TO-DATE SYSTEMS

☐ Hire Home Inspector [*before purchase*]

☐ Electrical

☐ A/C

☐ Heating

☐ Security

☐ Plumbing

☐ Water

☐ Sewer Insulation

ROOF

Y N

☐☐ Sagging Roof Line?

☐☐ Discoloration?

☐☐ Holes?

FOUNDATION, DRIVEWAY, & POOL

FOUNDATION

☐ Visible Cracks? _____________

DRIVEWAY

☐ Visible Cracks? _____________

POOL

☐ Visible Cracks? _____________

☐ Above Ground? _____________

GARAGE

Y N

☐☐ Functional - Manual?

☐☐ Functional - Remote?

☐ N/A

SIDING

Y N

☐☐ Paint Peeling?

☐☐ Cracks/Splits?

LANDSCAPING & CURB APPEAL

☐ Trees - Condition?

____

☐ Lawn [*front*] - Condition?

____

☐ Lawn [*back*] - Condition?

____

☐ Fences - Condition?

____

☐ Landscaping - Condition?

____

29

PROPERTY INFORMATION

ADDRESS	
BEDROOMS		**BATHROOMS**		**Sq. Ft.**	
LOT SIZE		**YEAR BUILT**		**SCHOOL DISTRICT**	
ANNUAL TAX		**PRICE**	

REALTOR INFORMATION

NAME	
AGENCY	
PHONE	
EMAIL	

NOTES AND REMINDERS

INSPECTION CHECKLIST

INTERIOR

FLOORING, WINDOWS & CEILING

FLOOR

☐ Age?

☐ Condition? _____________

WINDOWS

☐ Condition? _____________

CEILING

☐ Condition? _____________

ROOMS

Y N

☐☐ Natural Lighting?

☐☐ Even Floors?

☐☐ Smoke Detectors?

☐☐ Carbon Monoxide Detector?

WALLS

Y N

☐☐ Stains?

☐☐ Need Re-painting?

☐☐ Soundproof?

STAIRS

Y N

☐☐ Creaky?

☐☐ Signs of Damage?

DOORS

Y N

☐☐ Open & Close Property

☐☐ Weather Proofed

☐☐ Working Doorbell

BATHROOM

Y N

☐☐ Stain-free?

☐☐ Mildew/Mold-free?

☐☐ Leak-free?

☐☐ Cabinet & Storage Space?

☐☐ Working Fans?

☐☐ Functioning Toilet?

KITCHEN

Y N

☐☐ Stain-free?

☐☐ Mildew/Mold-free?

☐☐ Leak-free?

☐☐ Cabinet & Storage Space?

☐☐ Working Fans?

☐☐ Working Garbage Disposal?

EXTERIOR

UP-TO-DATE SYSTEMS

☐ Hire Home Inspector [*before purchase*]

☐ Electrical

☐ A/C

☐ Heating

☐ Security

☐ Plumbing

☐ Water

☐ Sewer Insulation

ROOF

Y N

☐☐ Sagging Roof Line?

☐☐ Discoloration?

☐☐ Holes?

FOUNDATION, DRIVEWAY, & POOL

FOUNDATION

☐ Visible Cracks? _____________

DRIVEWAY

☐ Visible Cracks? _____________

POOL

☐ Visible Cracks? _____________

☐ Above Ground? _____________

GARAGE

Y N

☐☐ Functional - Manual?

☐☐ Functional - Remote?

☐ N/A

SIDING

Y N

☐☐ Paint Peeling?

☐☐ Cracks/Splits?

LANDSCAPING & CURB APPEAL

☐ Trees - Condition?

____

☐ Lawn [*front*] - Condition?

____

☐ Lawn [*back*] - Condition?

____

☐ Fences - Condition?

____

☐ Landscaping - Condition?

____

30

PROPERTY INFORMATION

ADDRESS						
BEDROOMS		BATHROOMS		Sq. Ft.		
LOT SIZE		YEAR BUILT		SCHOOL DISTRICT		
ANNUAL TAX		PRICE				

REALTOR INFORMATION

NAME	
AGENCY	
PHONE	
EMAIL	

NOTES AND REMINDERS

INSPECTION CHECKLIST

INTERIOR

FLOORING, WINDOWS & CEILING

FLOOR
- ☐ Age?
- ☐ Condition? ___________

WINDOWS
- ☐ Condition? ___________

CEILING
- ☐ Condition? ___________

ROOMS

Y N
- ☐☐ Natural Lighting?
- ☐☐ Even Floors?
- ☐☐ Smoke Detectors?
- ☐☐ Carbon Monoxide Detector?

WALLS

Y N
- ☐☐ Stains?
- ☐☐ Need Re-painting?
- ☐☐ Soundproof?

STAIRS

Y N
- ☐☐ Creaky?
- ☐☐ Signs of Damage?

DOORS

Y N
- ☐☐ Open & Close Property
- ☐☐ Weather Proofed
- ☐☐ Working Doorbell

BATHROOM

Y N
- ☐☐ Stain-free?
- ☐☐ Mildew/Mold-free?
- ☐☐ Leak-free?
- ☐☐ Cabinet & Storage Space?
- ☐☐ Working Fans?
- ☐☐ Functioning Toilet?

KITCHEN

Y N
- ☐☐ Stain-free?
- ☐☐ Mildew/Mold-free?
- ☐☐ Leak-free?
- ☐☐ Cabinet & Storage Space?
- ☐☐ Working Fans?
- ☐☐ Working Garbage Disposal?

EXTERIOR

UP-TO-DATE SYSTEMS

- ☐ Hire Home Inspector [*before purchase*]
- ☐ Electrical
- ☐ A/C
- ☐ Heating
- ☐ Security
- ☐ Plumbing
- ☐ Water
- ☐ Sewer Insulation

ROOF

Y N
- ☐☐ Sagging Roof Line?
- ☐☐ Discoloration?
- ☐☐ Holes?

FOUNDATION, DRIVEWAY, & POOL

FOUNDATION
- ☐ Visible Cracks? ___________

DRIVEWAY
- ☐ Visible Cracks? ___________

POOL
- ☐ Visible Cracks? ___________
- ☐ Above Ground? ___________

GARAGE

Y N
- ☐☐ Functional - Manual?
- ☐☐ Functional - Remote?
- ☐ N/A

SIDING

Y N
- ☐☐ Paint Peeling?
- ☐☐ Cracks/Splits?

LANDSCAPING & CURB APPEAL

- ☐ Trees - Condition?
____

- ☐ Lawn [*front*] - Condition?
____

- ☐ Lawn [*back*] - Condition?
____

- ☐ Fences - Condition?
____

- ☐ Landscaping - Condition?
____

31

PROPERTY INFORMATION

ADDRESS	
BEDROOMS		BATHROOMS		Sq. Ft.	
LOT SIZE		YEAR BUILT		SCHOOL DISTRICT	
ANNUAL TAX		PRICE	

REALTOR INFORMATION

NAME	
AGENCY	
PHONE	
EMAIL	

NOTES AND REMINDERS

INSPECTION CHECKLIST

INTERIOR

FLOORING, WINDOWS & CEILING

FLOOR

☐ Age?

☐ Condition? _______________

WINDOWS

☐ Condition? _______________

CEILING

☐ Condition? _______________

ROOMS

Y N

☐☐ Natural Lighting?

☐☐ Even Floors?

☐☐ Smoke Detectors?

☐☐ Carbon Monoxide Detector?

WALLS

Y N

☐☐ Stains?

☐☐ Need Re-painting?

☐☐ Soundproof?

STAIRS

Y N

☐☐ Creaky?

☐☐ Signs of Damage?

DOORS

Y N

☐☐ Open & Close Property

☐☐ Weather Proofed

☐☐ Working Doorbell

BATHROOM

Y N

☐☐ Stain-free?

☐☐ Mildew/Mold-free?

☐☐ Leak-free?

☐☐ Cabinet & Storage Space?

☐☐ Working Fans?

☐☐ Functioning Toilet?

KITCHEN

Y N

☐☐ Stain-free?

☐☐ Mildew/Mold-free?

☐☐ Leak-free?

☐☐ Cabinet & Storage Space?

☐☐ Working Fans?

☐☐ Working Garbage Disposal?

EXTERIOR

UP-TO-DATE SYSTEMS

☐ Hire Home Inspector [*before purchase*]

☐ Electrical

☐ A/C

☐ Heating

☐ Security

☐ Plumbing

☐ Water

☐ Sewer Insulation

ROOF

Y N

☐☐ Sagging Roof Line?

☐☐ Discoloration?

☐☐ Holes?

FOUNDATION, DRIVEWAY, & POOL

FOUNDATION

☐ Visible Cracks? _______________

DRIVEWAY

☐ Visible Cracks? _______________

POOL

☐ Visible Cracks? _______________

☐ Above Ground? _______________

GARAGE

Y N

☐☐ Functional - Manual?

☐☐ Functional - Remote?

☐ N/A

SIDING

Y N

☐☐ Paint Peeling?

☐☐ Cracks/Splits?

LANDSCAPING & CURB APPEAL

☐ Trees - Condition?

____

☐ Lawn [*front*] - Condition?

____

☐ Lawn [*back*] - Condition?

____

☐ Fences - Condition?

____

☐ Landscaping - Condition?

____

32

PROPERTY INFORMATION

ADDRESS	
BEDROOMS		BATHROOMS		Sq. Ft.	
LOT SIZE		YEAR BUILT		SCHOOL DISTRICT	
ANNUAL TAX		PRICE	

REALTOR INFORMATION

NAME	
AGENCY	
PHONE	
EMAIL	

NOTES AND REMINDERS

INSPECTION CHECKLIST

INTERIOR

FLOORING, WINDOWS & CEILING

FLOOR

☐ Age?

☐ Condition? _______________

WINDOWS

☐ Condition? _______________

CEILING

☐ Condition? _______________

ROOMS

Y N

☐☐ Natural Lighting?

☐☐ Even Floors?

☐☐ Smoke Detectors?

☐☐ Carbon Monoxide Detector?

WALLS

Y N

☐☐ Stains?

☐☐ Need Re-painting?

☐☐ Soundproof?

STAIRS

Y N

☐☐ Creaky?

☐☐ Signs of Damage?

DOORS

Y N

☐☐ Open & Close Property

☐☐ Weather Proofed

☐☐ Working Doorbell

BATHROOM

Y N

☐☐ Stain-free?

☐☐ Mildew/Mold-free?

☐☐ Leak-free?

☐☐ Cabinet & Storage Space?

☐☐ Working Fans?

☐☐ Functioning Toilet?

KITCHEN

Y N

☐☐ Stain-free?

☐☐ Mildew/Mold-free?

☐☐ Leak-free?

☐☐ Cabinet & Storage Space?

☐☐ Working Fans?

☐☐ Working Garbage Disposal?

EXTERIOR

UP-TO-DATE SYSTEMS

☐ Hire Home Inspector [*before purchase*]

☐ Electrical

☐ A/C

☐ Heating

☐ Security

☐ Plumbing

☐ Water

☐ Sewer Insulation

ROOF

Y N

☐☐ Sagging Roof Line?

☐☐ Discoloration?

☐☐ Holes?

FOUNDATION, DRIVEWAY, & POOL

FOUNDATION

☐ Visible Cracks? _______________

DRIVEWAY

☐ Visible Cracks? _______________

POOL

☐ Visible Cracks? _______________

☐ Above Ground? _______________

GARAGE

Y N

☐☐ Functional - Manual?

☐☐ Functional - Remote?

☐ N/A

SIDING

Y N

☐☐ Paint Peeling?

☐☐ Cracks/Splits?

LANDSCAPING & CURB APPEAL

☐ Trees - Condition?

____

☐ Lawn [*front*] - Condition?

____

☐ Lawn [*back*] - Condition?

____

☐ Fences - Condition?

____

☐ Landscaping - Condition?

____

33

PROPERTY INFORMATION

ADDRESS	
BEDROOMS		**BATHROOMS**		**Sq. Ft.**	
LOT SIZE		**YEAR BUILT**		**SCHOOL DISTRICT**	
ANNUAL TAX		**PRICE**	

REALTOR INFORMATION

NAME	
AGENCY	
PHONE	
EMAIL	

NOTES AND REMINDERS

INSPECTION CHECKLIST

INTERIOR

FLOORING, WINDOWS & CEILING

FLOOR
- [ ] Age?
- [ ] Condition? _____________

WINDOWS
- [ ] Condition? _____________

CEILING
- [ ] Condition? _____________

ROOMS

Y N
- [ ] [ ] Natural Lighting?
- [ ] [ ] Even Floors?
- [ ] [ ] Smoke Detectors?
- [ ] [ ] Carbon Monoxide Detector?

WALLS

Y N
- [ ] [ ] Stains?
- [ ] [ ] Need Re-painting?
- [ ] [ ] Soundproof?

STAIRS

Y N
- [ ] [ ] Creaky?
- [ ] [ ] Signs of Damage?

DOORS

Y N
- [ ] [ ] Open & Close Property
- [ ] [ ] Weather Proofed
- [ ] [ ] Working Doorbell

BATHROOM

Y N
- [ ] [ ] Stain-free?
- [ ] [ ] Mildew/Mold-free?
- [ ] [ ] Leak-free?
- [ ] [ ] Cabinet & Storage Space?
- [ ] [ ] Working Fans?
- [ ] [ ] Functioning Toilet?

KITCHEN

Y N
- [ ] [ ] Stain-free?
- [ ] [ ] Mildew/Mold-free?
- [ ] [ ] Leak-free?
- [ ] [ ] Cabinet & Storage Space?
- [ ] [ ] Working Fans?
- [ ] [ ] Working Garbage Disposal?

EXTERIOR

UP-TO-DATE SYSTEMS

- [ ] Hire Home Inspector [*before purchase*]
- [ ] Electrical
- [ ] A/C
- [ ] Heating
- [ ] Security
- [ ] Plumbing
- [ ] Water
- [ ] Sewer Insulation

ROOF

Y N
- [ ] [ ] Sagging Roof Line?
- [ ] [ ] Discoloration?
- [ ] [ ] Holes?

FOUNDATION, DRIVEWAY, & POOL

FOUNDATION
- [ ] Visible Cracks? _____________

DRIVEWAY
- [ ] Visible Cracks? _____________

POOL
- [ ] Visible Cracks? _____________
- [ ] Above Ground? _____________

GARAGE

Y N
- [ ] [ ] Functional - Manual?
- [ ] [ ] Functional - Remote?
- [ ] N/A

SIDING

Y N
- [ ] [ ] Paint Peeling?
- [ ] [ ] Cracks/Splits?

LANDSCAPING & CURB APPEAL

- [ ] Trees - Condition?

____

- [ ] Lawn [*front*] - Condition?

____

- [ ] Lawn [*back*] - Condition?

____

- [ ] Fences - Condition?

____

- [ ] Landscaping - Condition?

____

34

PROPERTY INFORMATION

ADDRESS	
BEDROOMS		BATHROOMS		Sq. Ft.	
LOT SIZE		YEAR BUILT		SCHOOL DISTRICT	
ANNUAL TAX		PRICE	

REALTOR INFORMATION

NAME	
AGENCY	
PHONE	
EMAIL	

NOTES AND REMINDERS

INSPECTION CHECKLIST

INTERIOR

FLOORING, WINDOWS & CEILING

FLOOR

☐ Age?

☐ Condition? ___________

WINDOWS

☐ Condition? ___________

CEILING

☐ Condition? ___________

ROOMS

Y N

☐☐ Natural Lighting?

☐☐ Even Floors?

☐☐ Smoke Detectors?

☐☐ Carbon Monoxide Detector?

WALLS

Y N

☐☐ Stains?

☐☐ Need Re-painting?

☐☐ Soundproof?

STAIRS

Y N

☐☐ Creaky?

☐☐ Signs of Damage?

DOORS

Y N

☐☐ Open & Close Property

☐☐ Weather Proofed

☐☐ Working Doorbell

BATHROOM

Y N

☐☐ Stain-free?

☐☐ Mildew/Mold-free?

☐☐ Leak-free?

☐☐ Cabinet & Storage Space?

☐☐ Working Fans?

☐☐ Functioning Toilet?

KITCHEN

Y N

☐☐ Stain-free?

☐☐ Mildew/Mold-free?

☐☐ Leak-free?

☐☐ Cabinet & Storage Space?

☐☐ Working Fans?

☐☐ Working Garbage Disposal?

EXTERIOR

UP-TO-DATE SYSTEMS

☐ Hire Home Inspector [*before purchase*]

☐ Electrical

☐ A/C

☐ Heating

☐ Security

☐ Plumbing

☐ Water

☐ Sewer Insulation

ROOF

Y N

☐☐ Sagging Roof Line?

☐☐ Discoloration?

☐☐ Holes?

FOUNDATION, DRIVEWAY, & POOL

FOUNDATION

☐ Visible Cracks? ___________

DRIVEWAY

☐ Visible Cracks? ___________

POOL

☐ Visible Cracks? ___________

☐ Above Ground? ___________

GARAGE

Y N

☐☐ Functional - Manual?

☐☐ Functional - Remote?

☐ N/A

SIDING

Y N

☐☐ Paint Peeling?

☐☐ Cracks/Splits?

LANDSCAPING & CURB APPEAL

☐ Trees - Condition?

____

☐ Lawn [*front*] - Condition?

____

☐ Lawn [*back*] - Condition?

____

☐ Fences - Condition?

____

☐ Landscaping - Condition?

____

35

PROPERTY INFORMATION

ADDRESS	
BEDROOMS		BATHROOMS		Sq. Ft.	
LOT SIZE		YEAR BUILT		SCHOOL DISTRICT	
ANNUAL TAX		PRICE	

REALTOR INFORMATION

NAME	
AGENCY	
PHONE	
EMAIL	

NOTES AND REMINDERS

INSPECTION CHECKLIST

INTERIOR

FLOORING, WINDOWS & CEILING

FLOOR
- ☐ Age?
- ☐ Condition? _____________

WINDOWS
- ☐ Condition? _____________

CEILING
- ☐ Condition? _____________

ROOMS

Y N
- ☐☐ Natural Lighting?
- ☐☐ Even Floors?
- ☐☐ Smoke Detectors?
- ☐☐ Carbon Monoxide Detector?

WALLS

Y N
- ☐☐ Stains?
- ☐☐ Need Re-painting?
- ☐☐ Soundproof?

STAIRS

Y N
- ☐☐ Creaky?
- ☐☐ Signs of Damage?

DOORS

Y N
- ☐☐ Open & Close Property
- ☐☐ Weather Proofed
- ☐☐ Working Doorbell

BATHROOM

Y N
- ☐☐ Stain-free?
- ☐☐ Mildew/Mold-free?
- ☐☐ Leak-free?
- ☐☐ Cabinet & Storage Space?
- ☐☐ Working Fans?
- ☐☐ Functioning Toilet?

KITCHEN

Y N
- ☐☐ Stain-free?
- ☐☐ Mildew/Mold-free?
- ☐☐ Leak-free?
- ☐☐ Cabinet & Storage Space?
- ☐☐ Working Fans?
- ☐☐ Working Garbage Disposal?

EXTERIOR

UP-TO-DATE SYSTEMS

- ☐ Hire Home Inspector [*before purchase*]
- ☐ Electrical
- ☐ A/C
- ☐ Heating
- ☐ Security
- ☐ Plumbing
- ☐ Water
- ☐ Sewer Insulation

ROOF

Y N
- ☐☐ Sagging Roof Line?
- ☐☐ Discoloration?
- ☐☐ Holes?

FOUNDATION, DRIVEWAY, & POOL

FOUNDATION
- ☐ Visible Cracks? _____________

DRIVEWAY
- ☐ Visible Cracks? _____________

POOL
- ☐ Visible Cracks? _____________
- ☐ Above Ground? _____________

GARAGE

Y N
- ☐☐ Functional - Manual?
- ☐☐ Functional - Remote?
- ☐ N/A

SIDING

Y N
- ☐☐ Paint Peeling?
- ☐☐ Cracks/Splits?

LANDSCAPING & CURB APPEAL

- ☐ Trees - Condition?

____

- ☐ Lawn [*front*] - Condition?

____

- ☐ Lawn [*back*] - Condition?

____

- ☐ Fences - Condition?

____

- ☐ Landscaping - Condition?

____

36

PROPERTY INFORMATION

ADDRESS					
BEDROOMS		BATHROOMS		Sq. Ft.	
LOT SIZE		YEAR BUILT		SCHOOL DISTRICT	
ANNUAL TAX		PRICE			

REALTOR INFORMATION

NAME	
AGENCY	
PHONE	
EMAIL	

NOTES AND REMINDERS

INSPECTION CHECKLIST

INTERIOR

FLOORING, WINDOWS & CEILING

FLOOR
- [ ] Age?
- [ ] Condition? _______________

WINDOWS
- [ ] Condition? _______________

CEILING
- [ ] Condition? _______________

ROOMS

Y N
- [ ] [ ] Natural Lighting?
- [ ] [ ] Even Floors?
- [ ] [ ] Smoke Detectors?
- [ ] [ ] Carbon Monoxide Detector?

WALLS

Y N
- [ ] [ ] Stains?
- [ ] [ ] Need Re-painting?
- [ ] [ ] Soundproof?

STAIRS

Y N
- [ ] [ ] Creaky?
- [ ] [ ] Signs of Damage?

DOORS

Y N
- [ ] [ ] Open & Close Property
- [ ] [ ] Weather Proofed
- [ ] [ ] Working Doorbell

BATHROOM

Y N
- [ ] [ ] Stain-free?
- [ ] [ ] Mildew/Mold-free?
- [ ] [ ] Leak-free?
- [ ] [ ] Cabinet & Storage Space?
- [ ] [ ] Working Fans?
- [ ] [ ] Functioning Toilet?

KITCHEN

Y N
- [ ] [ ] Stain-free?
- [ ] [ ] Mildew/Mold-free?
- [ ] [ ] Leak-free?
- [ ] [ ] Cabinet & Storage Space?
- [ ] [ ] Working Fans?
- [ ] [ ] Working Garbage Disposal?

EXTERIOR

UP-TO-DATE SYSTEMS

- [ ] Hire Home Inspector [*before purchase*]
- [ ] Electrical
- [ ] A/C
- [ ] Heating
- [ ] Security
- [ ] Plumbing
- [ ] Water
- [ ] Sewer Insulation

ROOF

Y N
- [ ] [ ] Sagging Roof Line?
- [ ] [ ] Discoloration?
- [ ] [ ] Holes?

FOUNDATION, DRIVEWAY, & POOL

FOUNDATION
- [ ] Visible Cracks? _____________

DRIVEWAY
- [ ] Visible Cracks? _____________

POOL
- [ ] Visible Cracks? _____________
- [ ] Above Ground? _____________

GARAGE

Y N
- [ ] [ ] Functional - Manual?
- [ ] [ ] Functional - Remote?
- [ ] N/A

SIDING

Y N
- [ ] [ ] Paint Peeling?
- [ ] [ ] Cracks/Splits?

LANDSCAPING & CURB APPEAL

- [ ] Trees - Condition?

  ____

- [ ] Lawn [*front*] - Condition?

  ____

- [ ] Lawn [*back*] - Condition?

  ____

- [ ] Fences - Condition?

  ____

- [ ] Landscaping - Condition?

  ____

37

PROPERTY INFORMATION

ADDRESS	
BEDROOMS		**BATHROOMS**		**Sq. Ft.**	
LOT SIZE		**YEAR BUILT**		**SCHOOL DISTRICT**	
ANNUAL TAX		**PRICE**	

REALTOR INFORMATION

NAME	
AGENCY	
PHONE	
EMAIL	

NOTES AND REMINDERS

INSPECTION CHECKLIST

INTERIOR

FLOORING, WINDOWS & CEILING

FLOOR

☐ Age?

☐ Condition? _____________

WINDOWS

☐ Condition? _____________

CEILING

☐ Condition? _____________

ROOMS

Y N

☐☐ Natural Lighting?

☐☐ Even Floors?

☐☐ Smoke Detectors?

☐☐ Carbon Monoxide Detector?

WALLS

Y N

☐☐ Stains?

☐☐ Need Re-painting?

☐☐ Soundproof?

STAIRS

Y N

☐☐ Creaky?

☐☐ Signs of Damage?

DOORS

Y N

☐☐ Open & Close Property

☐☐ Weather Proofed

☐☐ Working Doorbell

BATHROOM

Y N

☐☐ Stain-free?

☐☐ Mildew/Mold-free?

☐☐ Leak-free?

☐☐ Cabinet & Storage Space?

☐☐ Working Fans?

☐☐ Functioning Toilet?

KITCHEN

Y N

☐☐ Stain-free?

☐☐ Mildew/Mold-free?

☐☐ Leak-free?

☐☐ Cabinet & Storage Space?

☐☐ Working Fans?

☐☐ Working Garbage Disposal?

EXTERIOR

UP-TO-DATE SYSTEMS

☐ Hire Home Inspector [*before purchase*]

☐ Electrical

☐ A/C

☐ Heating

☐ Security

☐ Plumbing

☐ Water

☐ Sewer Insulation

ROOF

Y N

☐☐ Sagging Roof Line?

☐☐ Discoloration?

☐☐ Holes?

FOUNDATION, DRIVEWAY, & POOL

FOUNDATION

☐ Visible Cracks? _____________

DRIVEWAY

☐ Visible Cracks? _____________

POOL

☐ Visible Cracks? _____________

☐ Above Ground? _____________

GARAGE

Y N

☐☐ Functional - Manual?

☐☐ Functional - Remote?

☐ N/A

SIDING

Y N

☐☐ Paint Peeling?

☐☐ Cracks/Splits?

LANDSCAPING & CURB APPEAL

☐ Trees - Condition?

____

☐ Lawn [*front*] - Condition?

____

☐ Lawn [*back*] - Condition?

____

☐ Fences - Condition?

____

☐ Landscaping - Condition?

____

38

PROPERTY INFORMATION

ADDRESS	
BEDROOMS		BATHROOMS		Sq. Ft.	
LOT SIZE		YEAR BUILT		SCHOOL DISTRICT	
ANNUAL TAX		PRICE	

REALTOR INFORMATION

NAME	
AGENCY	
PHONE	
EMAIL	

NOTES AND REMINDERS

INSPECTION CHECKLIST

INTERIOR

FLOORING, WINDOWS & CEILING

FLOOR

☐ Age?

☐ Condition? _______________

WINDOWS

☐ Condition? _______________

CEILING

☐ Condition? _______________

ROOMS

Y N

☐☐ Natural Lighting?

☐☐ Even Floors?

☐☐ Smoke Detectors?

☐☐ Carbon Monoxide Detector?

WALLS

Y N

☐☐ Stains?

☐☐ Need Re-painting?

☐☐ Soundproof?

STAIRS

Y N

☐☐ Creaky?

☐☐ Signs of Damage?

DOORS

Y N

☐☐ Open & Close Property

☐☐ Weather Proofed

☐☐ Working Doorbell

BATHROOM

Y N

☐☐ Stain-free?

☐☐ Mildew/Mold-free?

☐☐ Leak-free?

☐☐ Cabinet & Storage Space?

☐☐ Working Fans?

☐☐ Functioning Toilet?

KITCHEN

Y N

☐☐ Stain-free?

☐☐ Mildew/Mold-free?

☐☐ Leak-free?

☐☐ Cabinet & Storage Space?

☐☐ Working Fans?

☐☐ Working Garbage Disposal?

EXTERIOR

UP-TO-DATE SYSTEMS

☐ Hire Home Inspector [*before purchase*]

☐ Electrical

☐ A/C

☐ Heating

☐ Security

☐ Plumbing

☐ Water

☐ Sewer Insulation

ROOF

Y N

☐☐ Sagging Roof Line?

☐☐ Discoloration?

☐☐ Holes?

FOUNDATION, DRIVEWAY, & POOL

FOUNDATION

☐ Visible Cracks? _____________

DRIVEWAY

☐ Visible Cracks? _____________

POOL

☐ Visible Cracks? _____________

☐ Above Ground? _____________

GARAGE

Y N

☐☐ Functional - Manual?

☐☐ Functional - Remote?

☐ N/A

SIDING

Y N

☐☐ Paint Peeling?

☐☐ Cracks/Splits?

LANDSCAPING & CURB APPEAL

☐ Trees - Condition?

____

☐ Lawn [*front*] - Condition?

____

☐ Lawn [*back*] - Condition?

____

☐ Fences - Condition?

____

☐ Landscaping - Condition?

____

39

PROPERTY INFORMATION

ADDRESS	
BEDROOMS		BATHROOMS		Sq. Ft.	
LOT SIZE		YEAR BUILT		SCHOOL DISTRICT	
ANNUAL TAX		PRICE	

REALTOR INFORMATION

NAME	
AGENCY	
PHONE	
EMAIL	

NOTES AND REMINDERS

INSPECTION CHECKLIST

INTERIOR

FLOORING, WINDOWS & CEILING

FLOOR
- ☐ Age?
- ☐ Condition? ____________

WINDOWS
- ☐ Condition? ____________

CEILING
- ☐ Condition? ____________

ROOMS

Y N
- ☐☐ Natural Lighting?
- ☐☐ Even Floors?
- ☐☐ Smoke Detectors?
- ☐☐ Carbon Monoxide Detector?

WALLS

Y N
- ☐☐ Stains?
- ☐☐ Need Re-painting?
- ☐☐ Soundproof?

STAIRS

Y N
- ☐☐ Creaky?
- ☐☐ Signs of Damage?

DOORS

Y N
- ☐☐ Open & Close Property
- ☐☐ Weather Proofed
- ☐☐ Working Doorbell

BATHROOM

Y N
- ☐☐ Stain-free?
- ☐☐ Mildew/Mold-free?
- ☐☐ Leak-free?
- ☐☐ Cabinet & Storage Space?
- ☐☐ Working Fans?
- ☐☐ Functioning Toilet?

KITCHEN

Y N
- ☐☐ Stain-free?
- ☐☐ Mildew/Mold-free?
- ☐☐ Leak-free?
- ☐☐ Cabinet & Storage Space?
- ☐☐ Working Fans?
- ☐☐ Working Garbage Disposal?

EXTERIOR

UP-TO-DATE SYSTEMS

- ☐ Hire Home Inspector [*before purchase*]
- ☐ Electrical
- ☐ A/C
- ☐ Heating
- ☐ Security
- ☐ Plumbing
- ☐ Water
- ☐ Sewer Insulation

ROOF

Y N
- ☐☐ Sagging Roof Line?
- ☐☐ Discoloration?
- ☐☐ Holes?

FOUNDATION, DRIVEWAY, & POOL

FOUNDATION
- ☐ Visible Cracks? ____________

DRIVEWAY
- ☐ Visible Cracks? ____________

POOL
- ☐ Visible Cracks? ____________
- ☐ Above Ground? ____________

GARAGE

Y N
- ☐☐ Functional - Manual?
- ☐☐ Functional - Remote?
- ☐ N/A

SIDING

Y N
- ☐☐ Paint Peeling?
- ☐☐ Cracks/Splits?

LANDSCAPING & CURB APPEAL

- ☐ Trees - Condition?
____

- ☐ Lawn [*front*] - Condition?
____

- ☐ Lawn [*back*] - Condition?
____

- ☐ Fences - Condition?
____

- ☐ Landscaping - Condition?
____

40

PROPERTY INFORMATION

ADDRESS	
BEDROOMS		BATHROOMS		Sq. Ft.	
LOT SIZE		YEAR BUILT		SCHOOL DISTRICT	
ANNUAL TAX		PRICE	

REALTOR INFORMATION

NAME	
AGENCY	
PHONE	
EMAIL	

NOTES AND REMINDERS

INSPECTION CHECKLIST

INTERIOR

FLOORING, WINDOWS & CEILING

FLOOR
- ☐ Age?
- ☐ Condition? ___________

WINDOWS
- ☐ Condition? ___________

CEILING
- ☐ Condition? ___________

ROOMS

Y N
- ☐☐ Natural Lighting?
- ☐☐ Even Floors?
- ☐☐ Smoke Detectors?
- ☐☐ Carbon Monoxide Detector?

WALLS

Y N
- ☐☐ Stains?
- ☐☐ Need Re-painting?
- ☐☐ Soundproof?

STAIRS

Y N
- ☐☐ Creaky?
- ☐☐ Signs of Damage?

DOORS

Y N
- ☐☐ Open & Close Property
- ☐☐ Weather Proofed
- ☐☐ Working Doorbell

BATHROOM

Y N
- ☐☐ Stain-free?
- ☐☐ Mildew/Mold-free?
- ☐☐ Leak-free?
- ☐☐ Cabinet & Storage Space?
- ☐☐ Working Fans?
- ☐☐ Functioning Toilet?

KITCHEN

Y N
- ☐☐ Stain-free?
- ☐☐ Mildew/Mold-free?
- ☐☐ Leak-free?
- ☐☐ Cabinet & Storage Space?
- ☐☐ Working Fans?
- ☐☐ Working Garbage Disposal?

EXTERIOR

UP-TO-DATE SYSTEMS

- ☐ Hire Home Inspector [*before purchase*]
- ☐ Electrical
- ☐ A/C
- ☐ Heating
- ☐ Security
- ☐ Plumbing
- ☐ Water
- ☐ Sewer Insulation

ROOF

Y N
- ☐☐ Sagging Roof Line?
- ☐☐ Discoloration?
- ☐☐ Holes?

FOUNDATION, DRIVEWAY, & POOL

FOUNDATION
- ☐ Visible Cracks? ___________

DRIVEWAY
- ☐ Visible Cracks? ___________

POOL
- ☐ Visible Cracks? ___________
- ☐ Above Ground? ___________

GARAGE

Y N
- ☐☐ Functional - Manual?
- ☐☐ Functional - Remote?
- ☐ N/A

SIDING

Y N
- ☐☐ Paint Peeling?
- ☐☐ Cracks/Splits?

LANDSCAPING & CURB APPEAL

- ☐ Trees - Condition?

  ____

- ☐ Lawn [*front*] - Condition?

  ____

- ☐ Lawn [*back*] - Condition?

  ____

- ☐ Fences - Condition?

  ____

- ☐ Landscaping - Condition?

  ____

41

PROPERTY INFORMATION

ADDRESS					
BEDROOMS		BATHROOMS		Sq. Ft.	
LOT SIZE		YEAR BUILT		SCHOOL DISTRICT	
ANNUAL TAX		PRICE			

REALTOR INFORMATION

NAME	
AGENCY	
PHONE	
EMAIL	

NOTES AND REMINDERS

INSPECTION CHECKLIST

INTERIOR

FLOORING, WINDOWS & CEILING

FLOOR
- ☐ Age?
- ☐ Condition? _____________

WINDOWS
- ☐ Condition? _____________

CEILING
- ☐ Condition? _____________

ROOMS

Y N
- ☐☐ Natural Lighting?
- ☐☐ Even Floors?
- ☐☐ Smoke Detectors?
- ☐☐ Carbon Monoxide Detector?

WALLS

Y N
- ☐☐ Stains?
- ☐☐ Need Re-painting?
- ☐☐ Soundproof?

STAIRS

Y N
- ☐☐ Creaky?
- ☐☐ Signs of Damage?

DOORS

Y N
- ☐☐ Open & Close Property
- ☐☐ Weather Proofed
- ☐☐ Working Doorbell

BATHROOM

Y N
- ☐☐ Stain-free?
- ☐☐ Mildew/Mold-free?
- ☐☐ Leak-free?
- ☐☐ Cabinet & Storage Space?
- ☐☐ Working Fans?
- ☐☐ Functioning Toilet?

KITCHEN

Y N
- ☐☐ Stain-free?
- ☐☐ Mildew/Mold-free?
- ☐☐ Leak-free?
- ☐☐ Cabinet & Storage Space?
- ☐☐ Working Fans?
- ☐☐ Working Garbage Disposal?

EXTERIOR

UP-TO-DATE SYSTEMS

- ☐ Hire Home Inspector [*before purchase*]
- ☐ Electrical
- ☐ A/C
- ☐ Heating
- ☐ Security
- ☐ Plumbing
- ☐ Water
- ☐ Sewer Insulation

ROOF

Y N
- ☐☐ Sagging Roof Line?
- ☐☐ Discoloration?
- ☐☐ Holes?

FOUNDATION, DRIVEWAY, & POOL

FOUNDATION
- ☐ Visible Cracks? _____________

DRIVEWAY
- ☐ Visible Cracks? _____________

POOL
- ☐ Visible Cracks? _____________
- ☐ Above Ground? _____________

GARAGE

Y N
- ☐☐ Functional - Manual?
- ☐☐ Functional - Remote?
- ☐ N/A

SIDING

Y N
- ☐☐ Paint Peeling?
- ☐☐ Cracks/Splits?

LANDSCAPING & CURB APPEAL

- ☐ Trees - Condition?

____

- ☐ Lawn [*front*] - Condition?

____

- ☐ Lawn [*back*] - Condition?

____

- ☐ Fences - Condition?

____

- ☐ Landscaping - Condition?

____

42

PROPERTY INFORMATION

ADDRESS	
BEDROOMS		BATHROOMS		Sq. Ft.	
LOT SIZE		YEAR BUILT		SCHOOL DISTRICT	
ANNUAL TAX		**PRICE**	

REALTOR INFORMATION

NAME	
AGENCY	
PHONE	
EMAIL	

NOTES AND REMINDERS

INSPECTION CHECKLIST

INTERIOR

FLOORING, WINDOWS & CEILING

FLOOR

- ☐ Age?
- ☐ Condition? ___________

WINDOWS

- ☐ Condition? ___________

CEILING

- ☐ Condition? ___________

ROOMS

Y N

- ☐☐ Natural Lighting?
- ☐☐ Even Floors?
- ☐☐ Smoke Detectors?
- ☐☐ Carbon Monoxide Detector?

WALLS

Y N

- ☐☐ Stains?
- ☐☐ Need Re-painting?
- ☐☐ Soundproof?

STAIRS

Y N

- ☐☐ Creaky?
- ☐☐ Signs of Damage?

DOORS

Y N

- ☐☐ Open & Close Property
- ☐☐ Weather Proofed
- ☐☐ Working Doorbell

BATHROOM

Y N

- ☐☐ Stain-free?
- ☐☐ Mildew/Mold-free?
- ☐☐ Leak-free?
- ☐☐ Cabinet & Storage Space?
- ☐☐ Working Fans?
- ☐☐ Functioning Toilet?

KITCHEN

Y N

- ☐☐ Stain-free?
- ☐☐ Mildew/Mold-free?
- ☐☐ Leak-free?
- ☐☐ Cabinet & Storage Space?
- ☐☐ Working Fans?
- ☐☐ Working Garbage Disposal?

EXTERIOR

UP-TO-DATE SYSTEMS

- ☐ Hire Home Inspector [*before purchase*]
- ☐ Electrical
- ☐ A/C
- ☐ Heating
- ☐ Security
- ☐ Plumbing
- ☐ Water
- ☐ Sewer Insulation

ROOF

Y N

- ☐☐ Sagging Roof Line?
- ☐☐ Discoloration?
- ☐☐ Holes?

FOUNDATION, DRIVEWAY, & POOL

FOUNDATION

- ☐ Visible Cracks? ___________

DRIVEWAY

- ☐ Visible Cracks? ___________

POOL

- ☐ Visible Cracks? ___________
- ☐ Above Ground? ___________

GARAGE

Y N

- ☐☐ Functional - Manual?
- ☐☐ Functional - Remote?
- ☐ N/A

SIDING

Y N

- ☐☐ Paint Peeling?
- ☐☐ Cracks/Splits?

LANDSCAPING & CURB APPEAL

- ☐ Trees - Condition?
  ____
- ☐ Lawn [*front*] - Condition?
  ____
- ☐ Lawn [*back*] - Condition?
  ____
- ☐ Fences - Condition?
  ____
- ☐ Landscaping - Condition?
  ____

PROPERTY INFORMATION

ADDRESS	
BEDROOMS		BATHROOMS		Sq. Ft.	
LOT SIZE		YEAR BUILT		SCHOOL DISTRICT	
ANNUAL TAX		PRICE	

REALTOR INFORMATION

NAME	
AGENCY	
PHONE	
EMAIL	

NOTES AND REMINDERS

INSPECTION CHECKLIST

INTERIOR

FLOORING, WINDOWS & CEILING

FLOOR

- ☐ Age?
- ☐ Condition? ______________

WINDOWS

- ☐ Condition? ______________

CEILING

- ☐ Condition? ______________

ROOMS

Y N

- ☐☐ Natural Lighting?
- ☐☐ Even Floors?
- ☐☐ Smoke Detectors?
- ☐☐ Carbon Monoxide Detector?

WALLS

Y N

- ☐☐ Stains?
- ☐☐ Need Re-painting?
- ☐☐ Soundproof?

STAIRS

Y N

- ☐☐ Creaky?
- ☐☐ Signs of Damage?

DOORS

Y N

- ☐☐ Open & Close Property
- ☐☐ Weather Proofed
- ☐☐ Working Doorbell

BATHROOM

Y N

- ☐☐ Stain-free?
- ☐☐ Mildew/Mold-free?
- ☐☐ Leak-free?
- ☐☐ Cabinet & Storage Space?
- ☐☐ Working Fans?
- ☐☐ Functioning Toilet?

KITCHEN

Y N

- ☐☐ Stain-free?
- ☐☐ Mildew/Mold-free?
- ☐☐ Leak-free?
- ☐☐ Cabinet & Storage Space?
- ☐☐ Working Fans?
- ☐☐ Working Garbage Disposal?

EXTERIOR

UP-TO-DATE SYSTEMS

- ☐ Hire Home Inspector [*before purchase*]
- ☐ Electrical
- ☐ A/C
- ☐ Heating
- ☐ Security
- ☐ Plumbing
- ☐ Water
- ☐ Sewer Insulation

ROOF

Y N

- ☐☐ Sagging Roof Line?
- ☐☐ Discoloration?
- ☐☐ Holes?

FOUNDATION, DRIVEWAY, & POOL

FOUNDATION

- ☐ Visible Cracks? ___________

DRIVEWAY

- ☐ Visible Cracks? ___________

POOL

- ☐ Visible Cracks? ___________
- ☐ Above Ground? ___________

GARAGE

Y N

- ☐☐ Functional - Manual?
- ☐☐ Functional - Remote?
- ☐ N/A

SIDING

Y N

- ☐☐ Paint Peeling?
- ☐☐ Cracks/Splits?

LANDSCAPING & CURB APPEAL

- ☐ Trees - Condition?

  ____

- ☐ Lawn [*front*] - Condition?

  ____

- ☐ Lawn [*back*] - Condition?

  ____

- ☐ Fences - Condition?

  ____

- ☐ Landscaping - Condition?

  ____

44

PROPERTY INFORMATION

ADDRESS	
BEDROOMS		BATHROOMS		Sq. Ft.	
LOT SIZE		YEAR BUILT		SCHOOL DISTRICT	
ANNUAL TAX		PRICE	

REALTOR INFORMATION

NAME	
AGENCY	
PHONE	
EMAIL	

NOTES AND REMINDERS

INSPECTION CHECKLIST

INTERIOR

FLOORING, WINDOWS & CEILING

FLOOR
- ☐ Age?
- ☐ Condition? ____________

WINDOWS
- ☐ Condition? ____________

CEILING
- ☐ Condition? ____________

ROOMS

Y N
- ☐☐ Natural Lighting?
- ☐☐ Even Floors?
- ☐☐ Smoke Detectors?
- ☐☐ Carbon Monoxide Detector?

WALLS

Y N
- ☐☐ Stains?
- ☐☐ Need Re-painting?
- ☐☐ Soundproof?

STAIRS

Y N
- ☐☐ Creaky?
- ☐☐ Signs of Damage?

DOORS

Y N
- ☐☐ Open & Close Property
- ☐☐ Weather Proofed
- ☐☐ Working Doorbell

BATHROOM

Y N
- ☐☐ Stain-free?
- ☐☐ Mildew/Mold-free?
- ☐☐ Leak-free?
- ☐☐ Cabinet & Storage Space?
- ☐☐ Working Fans?
- ☐☐ Functioning Toilet?

KITCHEN

Y N
- ☐☐ Stain-free?
- ☐☐ Mildew/Mold-free?
- ☐☐ Leak-free?
- ☐☐ Cabinet & Storage Space?
- ☐☐ Working Fans?
- ☐☐ Working Garbage Disposal?

EXTERIOR

UP-TO-DATE SYSTEMS

- ☐ Hire Home Inspector [*before purchase*]
- ☐ Electrical
- ☐ A/C
- ☐ Heating
- ☐ Security
- ☐ Plumbing
- ☐ Water
- ☐ Sewer Insulation

ROOF

Y N
- ☐☐ Sagging Roof Line?
- ☐☐ Discoloration?
- ☐☐ Holes?

FOUNDATION, DRIVEWAY, & POOL

FOUNDATION
- ☐ Visible Cracks? __________

DRIVEWAY
- ☐ Visible Cracks? __________

POOL
- ☐ Visible Cracks? __________
- ☐ Above Ground? __________

GARAGE

Y N
- ☐☐ Functional - Manual?
- ☐☐ Functional - Remote?
- ☐ N/A

SIDING

Y N
- ☐☐ Paint Peeling?
- ☐☐ Cracks/Splits?

LANDSCAPING & CURB APPEAL

- ☐ Trees - Condition?

____

- ☐ Lawn [*front*] - Condition?

____

- ☐ Lawn [*back*] - Condition?

____

- ☐ Fences - Condition?

____

- ☐ Landscaping - Condition?

____

45

PROPERTY INFORMATION

ADDRESS					
BEDROOMS		BATHROOMS		Sq. Ft.	
LOT SIZE		YEAR BUILT		SCHOOL DISTRICT	
ANNUAL TAX		PRICE			

REALTOR INFORMATION

NAME	
AGENCY	
PHONE	
EMAIL	

NOTES AND REMINDERS

INSPECTION CHECKLIST

INTERIOR

FLOORING, WINDOWS & CEILING

FLOOR
- ☐ Age?
- ☐ Condition? _____________

WINDOWS
- ☐ Condition? _____________

CEILING
- ☐ Condition? _____________

ROOMS

Y N
- ☐☐ Natural Lighting?
- ☐☐ Even Floors?
- ☐☐ Smoke Detectors?
- ☐☐ Carbon Monoxide Detector?

WALLS

Y N
- ☐☐ Stains?
- ☐☐ Need Re-painting?
- ☐☐ Soundproof?

STAIRS

Y N
- ☐☐ Creaky?
- ☐☐ Signs of Damage?

DOORS

Y N
- ☐☐ Open & Close Property
- ☐☐ Weather Proofed
- ☐☐ Working Doorbell

BATHROOM

Y N
- ☐☐ Stain-free?
- ☐☐ Mildew/Mold-free?
- ☐☐ Leak-free?
- ☐☐ Cabinet & Storage Space?
- ☐☐ Working Fans?
- ☐☐ Functioning Toilet?

KITCHEN

Y N
- ☐☐ Stain-free?
- ☐☐ Mildew/Mold-free?
- ☐☐ Leak-free?
- ☐☐ Cabinet & Storage Space?
- ☐☐ Working Fans?
- ☐☐ Working Garbage Disposal?

EXTERIOR

UP-TO-DATE SYSTEMS

- ☐ Hire Home Inspector [*before purchase*]
- ☐ Electrical
- ☐ A/C
- ☐ Heating
- ☐ Security
- ☐ Plumbing
- ☐ Water
- ☐ Sewer Insulation

ROOF

Y N
- ☐☐ Sagging Roof Line?
- ☐☐ Discoloration?
- ☐☐ Holes?

FOUNDATION, DRIVEWAY, & POOL

FOUNDATION
- ☐ Visible Cracks? _____________

DRIVEWAY
- ☐ Visible Cracks? _____________

POOL
- ☐ Visible Cracks? _____________
- ☐ Above Ground? _____________

GARAGE

Y N
- ☐☐ Functional - Manual?
- ☐☐ Functional - Remote?
- ☐ N/A

SIDING

Y N
- ☐☐ Paint Peeling?
- ☐☐ Cracks/Splits?

LANDSCAPING & CURB APPEAL

- ☐ Trees - Condition?
____

- ☐ Lawn [*front*] - Condition?
____

- ☐ Lawn [*back*] - Condition?
____

- ☐ Fences - Condition?
____

- ☐ Landscaping - Condition?
____

46

PROPERTY INFORMATION

ADDRESS					
BEDROOMS		BATHROOMS		Sq. Ft.	
LOT SIZE		YEAR BUILT		SCHOOL DISTRICT	
ANNUAL TAX		PRICE			

REALTOR INFORMATION

NAME	
AGENCY	
PHONE	
EMAIL	

NOTES AND REMINDERS

INSPECTION CHECKLIST

INTERIOR

FLOORING, WINDOWS & CEILING

FLOOR

☐ Age?

☐ Condition? _____________

WINDOWS

☐ Condition? _____________

CEILING

☐ Condition? _____________

ROOMS

Y N

☐☐ Natural Lighting?

☐☐ Even Floors?

☐☐ Smoke Detectors?

☐☐ Carbon Monoxide Detector?

WALLS

Y N

☐☐ Stains?

☐☐ Need Re-painting?

☐☐ Soundproof?

STAIRS

Y N

☐☐ Creaky?

☐☐ Signs of Damage?

DOORS

Y N

☐☐ Open & Close Property

☐☐ Weather Proofed

☐☐ Working Doorbell

BATHROOM

Y N

☐☐ Stain-free?

☐☐ Mildew/Mold-free?

☐☐ Leak-free?

☐☐ Cabinet & Storage Space?

☐☐ Working Fans?

☐☐ Functioning Toilet?

KITCHEN

Y N

☐☐ Stain-free?

☐☐ Mildew/Mold-free?

☐☐ Leak-free?

☐☐ Cabinet & Storage Space?

☐☐ Working Fans?

☐☐ Working Garbage Disposal?

EXTERIOR

UP-TO-DATE SYSTEMS

☐ Hire Home Inspector [*before purchase*]

☐ Electrical

☐ A/C

☐ Heating

☐ Security

☐ Plumbing

☐ Water

☐ Sewer Insulation

ROOF

Y N

☐☐ Sagging Roof Line?

☐☐ Discoloration?

☐☐ Holes?

FOUNDATION, DRIVEWAY, & POOL

FOUNDATION

☐ Visible Cracks? _____________

DRIVEWAY

☐ Visible Cracks? _____________

POOL

☐ Visible Cracks? _____________

☐ Above Ground? _____________

GARAGE

Y N

☐☐ Functional - Manual?

☐☐ Functional - Remote?

☐ N/A

SIDING

Y N

☐☐ Paint Peeling?

☐☐ Cracks/Splits?

LANDSCAPING & CURB APPEAL

☐ Trees - Condition?

____

☐ Lawn [*front*] - Condition?

____

☐ Lawn [*back*] - Condition?

____

☐ Fences - Condition?

____

☐ Landscaping - Condition?

____

47

PROPERTY INFORMATION

ADDRESS					
BEDROOMS		BATHROOMS		Sq. Ft.	
LOT SIZE		YEAR BUILT		SCHOOL DISTRICT	
ANNUAL TAX			PRICE		

REALTOR INFORMATION

NAME	
AGENCY	
PHONE	
EMAIL	

NOTES AND REMINDERS

INSPECTION CHECKLIST

INTERIOR

FLOORING, WINDOWS & CEILING

FLOOR

☐ Age?

☐ Condition? _______________

WINDOWS

☐ Condition? _______________

CEILING

☐ Condition? _______________

ROOMS

Y N

☐☐ Natural Lighting?

☐☐ Even Floors?

☐☐ Smoke Detectors?

☐☐ Carbon Monoxide Detector?

WALLS

Y N

☐☐ Stains?

☐☐ Need Re-painting?

☐☐ Soundproof?

STAIRS

Y N

☐☐ Creaky?

☐☐ Signs of Damage?

DOORS

Y N

☐☐ Open & Close Property

☐☐ Weather Proofed

☐☐ Working Doorbell

BATHROOM

Y N

☐☐ Stain-free?

☐☐ Mildew/Mold-free?

☐☐ Leak-free?

☐☐ Cabinet & Storage Space?

☐☐ Working Fans?

☐☐ Functioning Toilet?

KITCHEN

Y N

☐☐ Stain-free?

☐☐ Mildew/Mold-free?

☐☐ Leak-free?

☐☐ Cabinet & Storage Space?

☐☐ Working Fans?

☐☐ Working Garbage Disposal?

EXTERIOR

UP-TO-DATE SYSTEMS

☐ Hire Home Inspector [*before purchase*]

☐ Electrical

☐ A/C

☐ Heating

☐ Security

☐ Plumbing

☐ Water

☐ Sewer Insulation

ROOF

Y N

☐☐ Sagging Roof Line?

☐☐ Discoloration?

☐☐ Holes?

FOUNDATION, DRIVEWAY, & POOL

FOUNDATION

☐ Visible Cracks? _______________

DRIVEWAY

☐ Visible Cracks? _______________

POOL

☐ Visible Cracks? _______________

☐ Above Ground? _______________

GARAGE

Y N

☐☐ Functional - Manual?

☐☐ Functional - Remote?

☐ N/A

SIDING

Y N

☐☐ Paint Peeling?

☐☐ Cracks/Splits?

LANDSCAPING & CURB APPEAL

☐ Trees - Condition?

____

☐ Lawn [*front*] - Condition?

____

☐ Lawn [*back*] - Condition?

____

☐ Fences - Condition?

____

☐ Landscaping - Condition?

____

48

PROPERTY INFORMATION

ADDRESS	
BEDROOMS		BATHROOMS		Sq. Ft.	
LOT SIZE		YEAR BUILT		SCHOOL DISTRICT	
ANNUAL TAX		PRICE	

REALTOR INFORMATION

NAME	
AGENCY	
PHONE	
EMAIL	

NOTES AND REMINDERS

INSPECTION CHECKLIST

INTERIOR

FLOORING, WINDOWS & CEILING

FLOOR

- ☐ Age?
- ☐ Condition? ____________

WINDOWS

- ☐ Condition? ____________

CEILING

- ☐ Condition? ____________

ROOMS

Y N

- ☐☐ Natural Lighting?
- ☐☐ Even Floors?
- ☐☐ Smoke Detectors?
- ☐☐ Carbon Monoxide Detector?

WALLS

Y N

- ☐☐ Stains?
- ☐☐ Need Re-painting?
- ☐☐ Soundproof?

STAIRS

Y N

- ☐☐ Creaky?
- ☐☐ Signs of Damage?

DOORS

Y N

- ☐☐ Open & Close Property
- ☐☐ Weather Proofed
- ☐☐ Working Doorbell

BATHROOM

Y N

- ☐☐ Stain-free?
- ☐☐ Mildew/Mold-free?
- ☐☐ Leak-free?
- ☐☐ Cabinet & Storage Space?
- ☐☐ Working Fans?
- ☐☐ Functioning Toilet?

KITCHEN

Y N

- ☐☐ Stain-free?
- ☐☐ Mildew/Mold-free?
- ☐☐ Leak-free?
- ☐☐ Cabinet & Storage Space?
- ☐☐ Working Fans?
- ☐☐ Working Garbage Disposal?

EXTERIOR

UP-TO-DATE SYSTEMS

- ☐ Hire Home Inspector [*before purchase*]
- ☐ Electrical
- ☐ A/C
- ☐ Heating
- ☐ Security
- ☐ Plumbing
- ☐ Water
- ☐ Sewer Insulation

ROOF

Y N

- ☐☐ Sagging Roof Line?
- ☐☐ Discoloration?
- ☐☐ Holes?

FOUNDATION, DRIVEWAY, & POOL

FOUNDATION

- ☐ Visible Cracks? __________

DRIVEWAY

- ☐ Visible Cracks? __________

POOL

- ☐ Visible Cracks? __________
- ☐ Above Ground? __________

GARAGE

Y N

- ☐☐ Functional - Manual?
- ☐☐ Functional - Remote?
- ☐ N/A

SIDING

Y N

- ☐☐ Paint Peeling?
- ☐☐ Cracks/Splits?

LANDSCAPING & CURB APPEAL

- ☐ Trees - Condition?

  ____

- ☐ Lawn [*front*] - Condition?

  ____

- ☐ Lawn [*back*] - Condition?

  ____

- ☐ Fences - Condition?

  ____

- ☐ Landscaping - Condition?

  ____

49

PROPERTY INFORMATION

ADDRESS	
BEDROOMS		BATHROOMS		Sq. Ft.	
LOT SIZE		YEAR BUILT		SCHOOL DISTRICT	
ANNUAL TAX		PRICE	

REALTOR INFORMATION

NAME	
AGENCY	
PHONE	
EMAIL	

NOTES AND REMINDERS

INSPECTION CHECKLIST

INTERIOR

FLOORING, WINDOWS & CEILING

FLOOR

- ☐ Age?
- ☐ Condition? _____________

WINDOWS

- ☐ Condition? _____________

CEILING

- ☐ Condition? _____________

ROOMS

Y N

- ☐☐ Natural Lighting?
- ☐☐ Even Floors?
- ☐☐ Smoke Detectors?
- ☐☐ Carbon Monoxide Detector?

WALLS

Y N

- ☐☐ Stains?
- ☐☐ Need Re-painting?
- ☐☐ Soundproof?

STAIRS

Y N

- ☐☐ Creaky?
- ☐☐ Signs of Damage?

DOORS

Y N

- ☐☐ Open & Close Property
- ☐☐ Weather Proofed
- ☐☐ Working Doorbell

BATHROOM

Y N

- ☐☐ Stain-free?
- ☐☐ Mildew/Mold-free?
- ☐☐ Leak-free?
- ☐☐ Cabinet & Storage Space?
- ☐☐ Working Fans?
- ☐☐ Functioning Toilet?

KITCHEN

Y N

- ☐☐ Stain-free?
- ☐☐ Mildew/Mold-free?
- ☐☐ Leak-free?
- ☐☐ Cabinet & Storage Space?
- ☐☐ Working Fans?
- ☐☐ Working Garbage Disposal?

EXTERIOR

UP-TO-DATE SYSTEMS

- ☐ Hire Home Inspector [*before purchase*]
- ☐ Electrical
- ☐ A/C
- ☐ Heating
- ☐ Security
- ☐ Plumbing
- ☐ Water
- ☐ Sewer Insulation

ROOF

Y N

- ☐☐ Sagging Roof Line?
- ☐☐ Discoloration?
- ☐☐ Holes?

FOUNDATION, DRIVEWAY, & POOL

FOUNDATION

- ☐ Visible Cracks? _____________

DRIVEWAY

- ☐ Visible Cracks? _____________

POOL

- ☐ Visible Cracks? _____________
- ☐ Above Ground? _____________

GARAGE

Y N

- ☐☐ Functional - Manual?
- ☐☐ Functional - Remote?
- ☐ N/A

SIDING

Y N

- ☐☐ Paint Peeling?
- ☐☐ Cracks/Splits?

LANDSCAPING & CURB APPEAL

- ☐ Trees - Condition? _____________
- ☐ Lawn [*front*] - Condition? _____________
- ☐ Lawn [*back*] - Condition? _____________
- ☐ Fences - Condition? _____________
- ☐ Landscaping - Condition? _____________

50

PROPERTY INFORMATION

ADDRESS					
BEDROOMS		BATHROOMS		Sq. Ft.	
LOT SIZE		YEAR BUILT		SCHOOL DISTRICT	
ANNUAL TAX		PRICE			

REALTOR INFORMATION

NAME	
AGENCY	
PHONE	
EMAIL	

NOTES AND REMINDERS

INSPECTION CHECKLIST

INTERIOR

FLOORING, WINDOWS & CEILING

FLOOR

☐ Age?

☐ Condition? _____________

WINDOWS

☐ Condition? _____________

CEILING

☐ Condition? _____________

ROOMS

Y N

☐☐ Natural Lighting?

☐☐ Even Floors?

☐☐ Smoke Detectors?

☐☐ Carbon Monoxide Detector?

WALLS

Y N

☐☐ Stains?

☐☐ Need Re-painting?

☐☐ Soundproof?

STAIRS

Y N

☐☐ Creaky?

☐☐ Signs of Damage?

DOORS

Y N

☐☐ Open & Close Property

☐☐ Weather Proofed

☐☐ Working Doorbell

BATHROOM

Y N

☐☐ Stain-free?

☐☐ Mildew/Mold-free?

☐☐ Leak-free?

☐☐ Cabinet & Storage Space?

☐☐ Working Fans?

☐☐ Functioning Toilet?

KITCHEN

Y N

☐☐ Stain-free?

☐☐ Mildew/Mold-free?

☐☐ Leak-free?

☐☐ Cabinet & Storage Space?

☐☐ Working Fans?

☐☐ Working Garbage Disposal?

EXTERIOR

UP-TO-DATE SYSTEMS

☐ Hire Home Inspector [*before purchase*]

☐ Electrical

☐ A/C

☐ Heating

☐ Security

☐ Plumbing

☐ Water

☐ Sewer Insulation

ROOF

Y N

☐☐ Sagging Roof Line?

☐☐ Discoloration?

☐☐ Holes?

FOUNDATION, DRIVEWAY, & POOL

FOUNDATION

☐ Visible Cracks? _____________

DRIVEWAY

☐ Visible Cracks? _____________

POOL

☐ Visible Cracks? _____________

☐ Above Ground? _____________

GARAGE

Y N

☐☐ Functional - Manual?

☐☐ Functional - Remote?

☐ N/A

SIDING

Y N

☐☐ Paint Peeling?

☐☐ Cracks/Splits?

LANDSCAPING & CURB APPEAL

☐ Trees - Condition?

____

☐ Lawn [*front*] - Condition?

____

☐ Lawn [*back*] - Condition?

____

☐ Fences - Condition?

____

☐ Landscaping - Condition?

____

www.ingramcontent.com/pod-product-compliance
Lightning Source LLC
Chambersburg PA
CBHW072104150726
47999CB00005B/1886